MY FIRST TIME IN CHARGE

Stop worrying – Start performing
Practical Guide for New Managers

DANIELE MATTEUCCI

authorHOUSE®

AuthorHouse™ UK
1663 Liberty Drive
Bloomington, IN 47403 USA
www.authorhouse.co.uk
Phone: UK TFN: 0800 0148641 (Toll Free inside the UK)
*   UK Local: 02036 956322 (+44 20 3695 6322 from outside the UK)*

Published by AuthorHouse 11/16/2020

ISBN: 978-1-5462-9934-9 (sc)
ISBN: 978-1-5462-9933-2 (e)

Contents

Introduction

This book is a practical guide that offers pragmatic tools and frameworks to new managers. It is the book I wished to have when I started my journey as a new manager with business responsibilities. I wrote it based on my real-life management experiences. I took notes for about four years of the lessons I learned during my first field assignment. I struggled, but finally I have been successful. I wished during my beginnings to have a mentor to coach me and help me to speed up my learning curve. I wish this book can be a valid practical guide to help others to reduce the stress and worries that inevitably happen when taking on a managerial role for the first time. At the same time, I wish to also offer new managers some help to deliver better and faster high performances.

The book is divided into two main areas: rational and emotional. I believe that a good manager must first of all master the rational part, but to become an excellent and complete manager, he or she cannot forget the emotional part of the job. Blending the rational and emotional parts will be a recipe for success and fulfillment.

PART I

RATIONAL

1

WHAT DO I MEAN BY RATIONAL?

When I started as a manager, I thought my job would have been simple: apply tools and principles to reach a business goal. After years of education in business, I came across so many tools that I thought my job would have been extremely easy. Those tools and principles were part of the rational part of the business, such as: setting targets and goals, key performance indicators; planning and control; review and tracking; following up on plans and decisions; on-time delivery and execution; accuracy; sales; prices and quantities; costs; profits; cash flow; credit and debits; standard operating procedures and 80/20 rule.

I studied accounting in high school, business administration at university and business strategy at post-graduate master. At fourteen years old, for the first time, I studied profit and loss statements and balance sheets. Since then, I have always been increasing my understanding and knowledge of these business topics.

My first job, at twenty-five, was in finance. I was involved in business controlling in the headquarters of a multinational eyewear company. Since the beginning I felt comfortable. In fact, I was working with all the tools I had learned in ten years of school. I worked on P&Ls for several subsidiaries. I was checking sales, prices, volumes, and profits. I became familiar with budgeting, forecasting, analysis of actual results, and gap analysis.

After almost five years in finance, I moved to demand planning department. It mainly focused on forecasting worldwide sales. Sales forecasts were shared with production and logistics to make sure the supply chain was set to deliver those volumes. I was also supporting my boss to guarantee the business in all geographies of the world was under control. I felt extremely at ease. I had ten years of business education and five years of experience in finance. Fifteen years with rational tools helped me analyze all the aspects of the business.

That solid base helped me do well in demand planning. I was good at analyzing actuals and predicting future sales. In my last year as Demand Planner, my team achieved a 0.03 percent sales variance versus the forecast we submitted in August — on almost sixty million products sold. A remarkable accuracy.

I spent eight years at headquarters (five years in finance and three in business planning). I spent eighteen years on the rational part of the business (ten at school and eight at work). Those eighteen years taught me how to plan, track, measure, and forecast a business in its dry numbers.

To be a solid manager, you need to master the rational part of the business. You cannot be a successful manager if you have gaps in that part. In this book, I present the necessary and helpful tools for my success. Tools are infinite, and the more you have in your toolbox, the better it is. You must understand the tools and be able to *really* utilize them at work. However, my first suggestion is to focus on the tools that *really* help you deliver. Focus on mastering a few tools instead of trying to learn many and not being able to use them at all. However, the second part of this book is related to the emotional aspect of being a manager. After my career in the corporate offices, I moved to a field assignment, and it has been there where I became a real manager. I understood that the rational tools were not enough. I learned that being manager is not as easy as I thought. I had to build other tools, emotional this time, not rational.

1.1 IT'S TIME FOR ACTION

- Which rational tools did you encounter in your education and work?
- Do you feel comfortable working with those tools?
- Do you feel gaps? If you feel comfortable, that's great. If you have some gaps, you must study, retrain, and close the gaps.
- Start making a list of your weak areas. Determine who can help you and commit to a date to start your gap-closing plan. If you can fix them by yourself, commit to a regular time each week until you close the weaknesses. If you cannot fix them alone, find someone who can help you.
- Which are the tools do you feel comfortable with? Write them down — and remember always to be confident when using them. Use them as much as possible.

2

TICK TOCK

The clock does not wait for you. When you are a manager, time is the only resource you cannot influence. To be an effective manager, you have to follow a timeline. You cannot speed up or slow down time. The only thing you can do is make your projects happen in the expected window or earlier. You must shorten the time between *ideas* and *actions*. Key questions to ask yourself:

- Are you fast at executing ideas?
- Is your team fast at executing ideas?
- How long will it take for an idea to become real action?
- How can you shorten that time?
- How can you generate excellent and applicable ideas?
- How can you start practical actions?

You can shorten the time from idea to action by defining who is doing what, when, where, and how. That is the essence of the action plan. You will find similar advice in many management and self-help books. It is an excellent piece of advice. You need to build a healthy obsession with the definition of the action plan. It is not enough to define which action to do. You need to identify all the elements: why, who, what, where, when, and how. If you do not have those answers, you do not have an action plan.

Below the tools I use in my work:

1. the purpose: the why
2. setting goals and clarifying: the bigger what for the medium and long term
3. the priority list of the month and quarter: the what in the short-term
4. the action plan: who is doing what by when
5. the next immediate action: how to kick-start the action
6. the after-action review: reflect on the progress

2.1 WHY DOES THE TEAM EXIST?

When I started as a Country Manager in Thailand, I was clear on the business objective. I spent eight years in the company before taking on the field role with management responsibilities. I knew which sales and profits goals the company was expecting. I was good at building budgets and a three-year plan for the new subsidiary I was going to manage. I knew all the leading key performance indicators. I thought that was enough, but I was wrong.

Maybe it was enough for me, but it was not enough for the forty employees of the organization. I spent my first year struggling to understand why we were so slow, why things never happened, why we missed deadlines, why people did not understand what was expected to happen, and why people did not deliver as I expected. I had many whys and no answers. I had to learn fast how to become successful, as a manager and as a team.

After a few months of managing, I had to change what I was doing. Otherwise, a clear failure was waiting for my team and me. What did I do? I started with setting and clarifying goals; utilized a priority list for the month and quarter; deployed the priorities into practical action plans; and started with action reviews. Things began to improve, and every time I introduced a new tool, I saw positive results. However, something was missing. After a year, I discovered what it was. It was another essential topic taught at business schools: vision and mission! This is why I present this tool as the first one of the rational part of this book. It must be the starting point of everything.

The first time I spoke about why we existed as a team and company was with my management line in an off-site leadership team. I prepared a few slides to introduce how everyone has a challenging mission, and at least one why. I used an example to show how missions can be extremely challenging. I spoke about the moon landing in 1969 and showed a picture of the three astronauts: Neil Armstrong, Buzz Aldrin, and Michael Collins. I said, "Those men had a mission to land on the moon, and we have a much less risky mission: we want to bring modernization in our industry." I explained what modernization meant to me.

At that time, my company did not have a formal vision and mission statement. I coined the expression "eyewear modernization." I showed a picture that described what I meant. Since most people remember pictures, I found a picture of an optical store upgraded in Malaysia. It was the first time I talked to my team about our purpose. The why was established, clear, and simple to remember. Through a picture.

That should be the first thing to do. Before setting goals, People must understand the bigger purpose of why they work every day and why they wake up every day. I asked a senior director to share her secret of business success. The answer was "purpose": find and share with people why they exist. Purpose fuels people's motivation in the long term. Goals can fuel motivation for a few years. I could not agree more.

Afterward, my HQ released the formal vision and mission statement. I discussed it with my employees in a quarterly meeting. I highlighted the key parts and sent them a link to the company's website. If you work for a company that does not have a vision statement, you cannot wait. You must prepare a purpose statement and share it with your team.

I do not have experience of building a mission statement with a team. Maybe it is possible. Get inputs from your team, as it could be effective to develop the mission statement with your employees, however, if you cannot get qualitative inputs, the mission statement must come from the company or you, the manager. Managers must show direction. Most employees want to know that their manager is a good one, and they want to think they are in good hands. If the manager is not able to articulate a mission statement, how could people believe they are in good hands?

The mission statement applies to every department. If you are managing a department, you must determine its purpose.

2.2 SETTING AND CLARIFYING GOALS

Setting goals is a traditional topic in business schools. Those goals must be shared with your team members. Another common theme about goals is that they should be SMART (specific, measurable, achievable, relevant, and timely).

- **Specific**. Very clearly defined what, why, by who, by when and where.
- **Measurable**. You need to be able to measure the key performance indicators.
- **Achievable**. Goals must be challenging, but still possible to achieve. If the goals seem impossible, no one will try.
- **Relevant**. The goal must be coherent with the mission statement and relevant for the company and the people. Teams and companies are made up of people. If the goal sparks a personal interest in people, they will feel more engaged and committed.
- **Timely**. The goal must have a specific time frame. When is the deadline?

The difficult part is making the SMART acronym alive and real every day! Continuously communicating goals is essential and requires a lot of discipline. For many managers, like you, it is usually easy to remember the goals and work toward them. You cannot think everyone on the team is like you. You need to dedicate time and efforts to continuously and frequently communicate the goals to your team members.

2.2.1 Stretch Goals

Goals must be SMART. Does having achievable goals mean you cannot dream big? You can imagine big — and that is why you can use stretch goals. You can define a stretch target, but you need to be careful. The stretch goal is more challenging than the goal itself, but it is still achievable. If your people put in more effort, skill, commitment, and motivation, it is possible to reach.

The stretch goal is the dream that can help you motivate your people to go above and beyond. The stretch goal should have a stretch incentive for your people. What will they get if they achieve the stretch goal? Special bonuses, special trips, or a tangible reward for their extra effort. If you are asking for a stretch goal, you need to provide a stretch incentive.

Tangible incentives are not the only thing that motivates people. People should feel proud and emotionally rewarded for their stretch achievements. When overachieving, people feel good about themselves. Everyone likes to be successful. People are happy to overachieve. However, if they overachieve the goal, you need to take care of your people and offer tangible rewards. In the future, your team will be committed to overachieve again. Make them feel proud about every overachievement. Celebrate it, let the positive emotions spread, and take care of their tangible rewards. Your team will be ready to overdeliver again in the future. If you miss one of the two, celebrating or rewarding, you are planting the seeds for an environment that does not value overachievement.

Another element to consider is the maturity, readiness, and performance level of your team. If you think your team is ready to aim for a stretch goal, then set it. If the team is not prepared to achieve, it may be better not to declare a stretch goal. When the team starts to perform better, start including stretch goals, not before.

Stretch goals can improve the performance of a team that is already performing well. For a team that is not performing, a stretch goal will be frustrating. What is the point of having a stretch goal than the team cannot achieve? It will be just another disappointment. Determine if it is the right time to identify a stretch goal. If it is not, do not implement a stretch goal just for the sake of saying you have identified one.

2.2.2 How to Communicate Goals

How do you communicate the goals? Find all the ways useful for you and your team. Think about which methods will be helpful — and don't limit yourself. Ask your team members how they prefer to be reminded about goals.

Prepare a document for sharing your goals. PowerPoint slides are easy to present in meetings, and you can email and use them in face-to-face meetings. You can also use them during reviews to your boss or your management team.

The document will need to state your key performance indicators. I am not talking about generic goals, for example, "growing the business." Instead, your document must have SMART goals, for example, "this year net sales increase x percent versus last year." You need to state all the key performance indicators for your organization and include everything you want to achieve. If you miss one, you cannot complain about it at the end of the year. If you do not include a goal, then the goal is not communicated, so there is no awareness from your team and no action taken to achieve it. Whatever you write, or not write, in that document is the beginning of a long chain. You have a responsibility to be clear about what you want to achieve. Everything starts with you.

A *goal-clarification map* is a simple two-axis graph. The horizontal line is *importance,* and the vertical line is *time.* Plot your yearly goals in the chart. Include the goals that must be achieved every month (in my case, it was sales, payments, profits, etc.). This graph is a simple way of visualizing to people how the year will be. It becomes an easy tool that will help people have a one-page simplification of the complexity around them. Everything will be clearer, and people will appreciate the clear timeline and be prepared.

Below an example of the goal-clarification map.

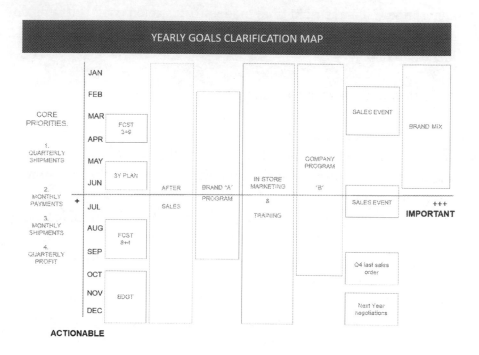

2.2.3 When to Communicate Goals

When should you communicate? The more frequently, the better. Remind your team about the goals whenever they are together. In the beginning, you will need to explain the details and spend more time going over them. After a while, your team will be familiar with goals — and you will spend less time going over the details. My practical suggestion is to communicate goals: every year, every quarter, every month, weekly or bi-weekly.

Every year, as soon as the budget is ready. If your company takes a long time to finalize the budget, then you cannot wait.

You have to give your best estimate of the objectives. It is not important to share the exact percentage growth or the absolute amount to reach. People need to know measurements and ranges. When the budget is available, you can communicate the final numbers. There is a well-known trade-off between accuracy and speed. You cannot wait for the most accurate number if that number is coming late. It is much better to get a reasonable estimate early on.

Every quarter, I have a quarterly off-site meeting with the management team. Again, share the current status, the objectives and remind your team about future goals. Every quarter or month, have one-on-one meetings with your team members. If you have managers reporting to you, ask them to clarify their goals in their one-on-one meetings with their team members.

Every month, have the team present its current progress against the goal. Use this occasion to remind team members about their goals. You can show the document you prepared and the goal-clarification map.

Every week or two, have meetings with smaller groups. I have a weekly or bi-weekly sales and finance meeting.

At the beginning of my career as a manager, I thought that sharing at the beginning of the year was enough. I soon realized how continually talking about objectives is important. You will start to see people get clear about what they have to do. You will begin to see how people feel safe and stable. People love certainty. When you always refer to the same goals in the same format, they become familiar with them. It becomes a routine. You will not risk surprises, for you and others, of having team members not being clear about what they have to do.

2.2.4 Where to Communicate Goals

Where should you communicate goals? Almost any location can work for talking about goals. In particular, I split into off-site and on-site locations.

> **Off-site** (outside the regular office or workplace) is the right solution for the beginning of the year and quarterly meetings. A few times a year is good to change environment. Changing the location by going somewhere new helps people to feel more interested. People spend at least eight hours a day in the office. Time to time is good to spend a few hours outside. When I was a kid, the teacher sometimes brought us outside when the weather was good. What a good feeling to get out of the classroom! It was only for an hour and a few times during the year, but I still remember those times. The same thing happens when you go off-site with your team.

> **On-site** works well for monthly and weekly meetings and one-on-one meetings. It is beneficial to use the same location for the same kinds of appointments. Use the same meeting room for weekly meetings. Use another meeting room for the monthly meetings. People get used to specific environments. It is a matter of building a habit and adding stability to a process. People will feel secure and comfortable in the same room (and even the same chair!).

2.2.5 Who to Communicate Goals

Who do you need to communicate to? The more people you communicate to, the better. Your organization will perform better when more people know about the goals you want to achieve. If you are the only one who knows the goals, you will be the only one to do all the job. If the management team knows the goals, other team members will help you. When everybody in the organization knows about the goals to achieve, every single person in the company will wake up every day knowing what to work for. In that situation, your working life will be much easier. I suggest you to follow the below routine to ensure everybody is clear on goals:

- All employees participate in a goals setting and review meeting at the beginning of the year and each quarter.
- All your direct reports, every month and not later than each quarter, participate in a goals setting and review meeting.

This routine ensures that everybody remembers goals. The monthly or quarterly meeting keeps the management line aligned. If you are the general manager, your team is your management line. You cannot override your management line by directly communicating every time to their teams. You need to respect your managers and empower them to manage their teams. However, from time to time, it is healthy to speak to the entire organization.

2.3 PRIORITY LIST OF THE MONTH AND QUARTER

Once the goals are set and communicated, you need to make sure people are clear on the priority of projects. Those key projects, or key priorities, are the milestones of the current month and current quarter. Working on those milestones will put you and your team in condition to achieve.

You must be clear on priorities for the month and the quarter. It is relatively easy to define priorities. What are the key projects that must be achieved this month and this quarter to stay on track toward achieving the overall yearly goal? Answer this question, rank the priorities, and prepare a document. You will share this *priority list* with your team.

You will decide if you want to share it with every employee or only with your direct reports. It depends on the effectiveness of your direct reports. If they are reliable and delivering great performances, share the priority list only with them. Let them deploy the priorities within their teams. If your direct reports are not performing well, you will be required to present the priorities to all employees.

- Share the priority list in the final week of the month so that people have time to reflect and include those priorities in their next plans. It could also be a great practice to have a monthly meeting with your direct reports and share the priority list.
- Share the priority list by email, following a monthly routine, with the same subject line and the same format. This practice will help you build a habit. In the body of the email, highlight a few of the priorities (a maximum of three) you want to highlight. You can highlight the most important priority, a new one or one you are not satisfied yet.
- Determine who is responsible for leading on the priority. You might want to identify the supporters as well. By doing so, you can empower the leader to ask others for help.
- Determine deadlines.
- Determine specific goals for each priority.
- Refer to the previous month's priority list and comment positively about achievements and what must be improved. If there is anything from the month before that has not progressed according to expectations, you need to call it out. List, in order, the core priorities, the top priorities, and then the high priorities.

Priority List Template (Action Plan)				
What	Who	When	How	Where

- Describe the action. What is the objective? What is the KPI?
- Who is responsible for the action?
- When is the deadline? All deadlines must be respected.
- How will the action be accomplished? Which steps, tools, and instructions are needed?

- Define where the action will take place.

There is only one principle to follow to make the action plan effective: be terrifically specific. For every question, there is a clear, detailed answer.

- What: You must declare the key performance indicator that will measure the achievement of the action.
- Who: You need to assign a clear responsibility to a person. It seems that Steve Jobs used the term *directly responsible individual* (Hakman, 2017). The responsibility is on a person — even if the project or action must be carried out by a team.
- When: A deadline is called a deadline because, after that, you are dead. You need to be clear to your team that you expect the action is completed by the due date.
- How: You need to make sure the *how* to carry on the action is defined. The essential requirement is to explain what the deliverable is. Depending on the situation, you have to adjust your style for explaining the how. If the capability of the DRI (directly responsible individual) and the overall team is not mature, you have to be extremely specific about how you want the action delivered. Offering more details will help the team follow your instructions. If the team is mature and has demonstrated ability to perform, it will be enough to define the deliverable.
- Where: You need to clarify where the action is supposed to happen. If you do not state where, actions may take place in the wrong location. In my job, we work on upgrading optical stores. For example, my company helped opticians improve fixtures, visual merchandising, and product displays. It is particularly important to define which shops by identifying store addresses. A generic definition, like "some stores in Bangkok," is meaningless. With an address, you will be able to start quickly.

The above could seem to some readers as micromanagement. But it is not. My western education is based on the principle of empowerment. I thought a manager should have shared and aligned objectives — and the team would have automatically engaged to deliver actions. I was in meetings with people and thought we had a great session because I talked about what we wanted to achieve. I looked at the people around the table and asked if everything was clear. I was available to help in case the team needed it. I thought I was doing the best job. When the deadlines approached, the job did not get done.

Empowerment does not mean just sharing a vision or a goal and then waiting. The more the team members are clear on all the elements of the action plan, the faster the execution will be. I learned this lesson by failing to meet deadlines, struggling to catch up, and rushing what should have been prepared much earlier.

I started to be more and more specific, defining all the elements. The definition could happen in a team meeting setting, where the team can specify all the points. The manager does not have to prepare all the details of the action plan. A team that is actively involved in preparing the action plan will be more lucid and more engaged. No one likes a top-down approach. It is much more useful to ask your team to develop the action plan. Your job is to review it to make sure the team is covering all areas. If some areas are missing, it is your job to complete them.

2.4 NEXT IMMEDIATE ACTION

How do you start these actions quickly? After defining the action plan, it is a matter of starting. It seems simple, but it is not!

After implementing the action plan, I felt better immediately. I thought *'everybody is clear on what must be done now!.'* In reality, I experienced a lack of speed in taking action. I could not understand why. I thought I had done everything right. I did not stop at setting goals. I also shared the action plan with the team! I thought that was enough, but it was not.

David Allen's book, *Getting Things Done,* talks about how to be more productive (Allen, 2015). The author speaks about the power of the *next immediate action.* What is the first action for you and others? For example, if the action is to upgrade ten stores by the end of next month, what will be the next immediate action? "Person X will prepare the list of ten stores by tomorrow and submit to person Y." That is the kick-starter. If you define the action plan and define the next immediate action, you can be pretty sure that your team will work at a reasonable speed.

I built a template for "next immediate action." I explained the topic to the team members, and they started to actively use the file. With clear actions and a short time horizon, I saw progress immediately. When actions slowed down, I could help the team to regain speed by defining the next immediate action.

Next Immediate Action				
What	Who	When	How	Where

- Refer to the bigger topic that you defined in the what of the action plan.
- Identify the person on your team who is responsible for the next immediate action.
- Identify the deadline. A deadline must be respected. In this case, it is short (no more than one week).
- Define how the action must be done. Which steps, tools, instructions must be used?
- Define where the action must be completed.

With this tool, you are slicing the bigger action in smaller pieces. By "chunking," the brain can better absorb small chunks of information. You can "cut the elephant in the room" by splitting a big problem into small parts. Reducing the problem to small parts will help you tackle the problem. Having many people in front of a big problem could result in more confusion. They may be overwhelmed and believe the problem has no solution. Splitting the problem into small parts will help reduce the complexity and facilitate finding a solution.

You and your team must start somewhere — as soon as possible. The next immediate action is a way of getting started. When the ball is rolling, it will be easier to move ahead. You can help your team by defining the action plan and providing the first input for the next immediate action.

Before using this simple tool, my to-do list was too long and I felt overwhelmed just knowing that I had so many tasks to complete. I was busy and feeling the day did not have enough hours. Since I started to use this tool instead, the results were amazing. The speed of execution started to improve dramatically and I started to feel in control of time. I was much more productive and I had more hours available.

The trick was simple — only two columns: *to-do list* and *next immediate action* — for every item on my list. I reviewed my to-do list at the end of every working day. The next day, I looked at the list and read from the next immediate action column. I just did whatever I had written down the night before. I was able to complete so many tasks, and I discovered the theory behind this tool. With a standard to-do list, items are identified, but your brain needs to think about what should be done. The mind is in thinking mode. When you write down the next immediate action instead, the brain immediately goes into execution mode. There is no more thinking. There is just doing. That is why the speed increases so much.

To-Do List	Next Immediate Action
Prepare a business plan for customer X	Send a meeting request to the sales director for next Tuesday to prepare the first draft together

Try it. You will see how it accelerates your capability to deliver. You will feel the pleasure of having extra free time. You will enjoy the feeling of completing so many things early in the morning.

2.5 ACTION REVIEW

How do you complete actions? The process must be concluded with the action review. The intent is to check the progress of the action plan. To complete this task is enough to take the action plan and judge if the progress is in line with expectations. I suggest using color codes to identify the status (red for far from completion; orange for improvements needed; green for on track).

Action Review Template					
What	Who	When	How	Where	Status

- What: describe the action. What's the objective? What is the key performance indicator?
- Who is responsible for the action?
- When is the deadline? The deadline must be respected.
- Define how the action must be done. Which steps, tools, instructions must be used?
- Define where the action must be completed.
- Include the color code and comments to quickly assess the progress

When a gap is identified, it is vital to implement corrective actions. Corrective action can be treated as the next immediate action. It is crucial to fix any gaps to give the right pace to the project and the team's attitude.

2.6 ACTION CHART

A company's organization chart shows how the company is organized by department, position, and team member. An organization chart has many positive aspects. It helps people clarify how the organization is structured. The other hidden message in the organization chart is who has the authority. The CEO is on the top and has the most authority. However, actions never follow authority. An action chart is an upside-down organization chart.

During my first year, I was struggling. Even if I was at the top of the organization chart in my subsidiary, I was not the one doing things. I was just one person, but thirty-nine other people were taking actions every day. Employees in the Finance Department were collecting payments from customers; salespeople were collecting sales orders; people in marketing were implementing activities in the stores; people in the Operations Department were ensuring shipments, and people in the Training Department were training employees and staff. I was really far from the action. My first-line managers were closer to the action than I was, but the ones making things happen were the employees. The faster you realize this, the faster you will understand that you are not the most important person in the company or your department. You are probably paid more than others if you are a general manager or a department manager, but you are not the most important person. When you look at it this way, you realize you are at the bottom of the organization. The most important people are your employees. You are there to serve them. You are there to build the conditions for them to succeed. You succeed as a manager if you can direct the energies of your employees in the right direction. You succeed if everyone in the organization can take the right action.

In a simplified organization chart, you find three main layers:

- CEO
- management line
- employees

In the Action Chart you find the same three main layers upside-down.

Employees make the actions, managers define the action plan and action review, and the general manager or CEO defines the company's purpose and priorities. I started looking at trees as a way to visualize the action chart:

- Flowers are the results. In some seasons, you have great flowers. In other seasons, there are not many flowers or none at all.
- The leaves are your employees. They are close to the final results (the flowers).
- The branches represent your management line. They carry the leaves.
- The trunk represents the general manager. It is at the bottom and sustains everything above it.

There are also a few other considerations when you look at the tree:

- Flowers and leaves make the tree beautiful — just as good results and employees make a good company.
- If the tree were made up of only the trunk or the branches, it would be boring.
- Flowers can be seasonal. The results will not always come in business, but the tree is still alive. Don't judge your organization only on results.
- The last point is about the roots. You don't see them when you imagine a tree. However, the tree does not exist without them. The roots represent the group your company is part of (systems, products, research, management, legal, fiscal, and shareholders).

What is behind you is extremely important in your job. If the roots are healthy, your chances to do well will increase.

2.7 ACTION LINE

Another way to imagine the actions that must be carried out is to imagine a train line, subway line, or bus line.
Every day, I took the Skytrain to my office in Bangkok (two stops from Ratchadamri to Chong Nonsi). I have done this for four years. One day, I looked at the rail line and had an a-ha moment. You can visualize your projects as a standalone line. Every station represents the key objectives and steps to accomplish.

The Action Line related to a customer, for example, could be as follow:

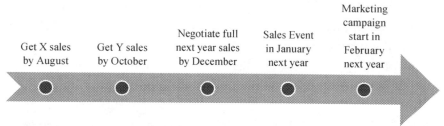

Very important to build your line to ensure that:

- The key success moments are defined.
- Only key events are identified.
- Time is clearly identified.
- The line is straight, in chronological order.
- There is one line for every department or main objectives.

Along time, follow the line. If you see that you are not going at the right speed, you must accelerate. If you missed a station, get back on track, and try to achieve the next one.

2.8 IT'S TIME FOR ACTION

Think about your situation.

The manager clearly defines the actions that need to be taken. It is not enough to share the goals and priorities with team members. It is also important to define all the elements of the action plan (who, where, what, when, where, and how). Did you do it? If not, it is helpful to prepare a template to share with all team members. Could this help with continuous alignment?

You have seen how important it is to find a way to start all the actions identified. The next immediate action helps you go into execution mode. You can influence your brain to think less and do more. Do you have an immediate action for every priority you have?

It is important for good managers to have a regular action review, which will help you identify what is going well and what is not. Taking corrective actions fast is the only way to catch up. Do you have regular debrief sessions?

Remember that the clock is ticking, and it is not going to wait for you. You will be either on time against your objectives or late. There are no other options.
You do not need only to do the right things, but you are required to do the right things at the right time. Are you doing the right things? Are you doing the right things at the right time?

3

PEOPLE

I s it easy to work with others? Are all people working for the greater good? It is easy to work with people you like, but what about the ones you don't? It is relatively easy to work with people with a similar background, nationality, religion, race, gender, age, culture. What about working with people diverse from you? What about working with people with higher or lower IQ than yours? And what about people with higher or lower EQ? What about people different from you? There is only one truth in the workplace: you will not be successful if you do not learn how to work with others.

3.1 IDEA-ACTION MATRIX

You cannot make things happen alone. You need the help of others. You can fall into one of two categories:

- Category 1: You are a solo player, you are great, and you don't like working with others. You might think working with others is not efficient, and you do better when working alone.
- Category 2: You like working with others, and you think it is more interesting, effective, and joyful to work together. You

might feel bored working alone, and your natural preference is to stay with others.

If you fall in category one, you should move quickly to category two. You will not be a successful manager if you continue to work alone. It is a simple math exercise. Do you think you can manage and lead a team without the help and consent of the people you manage? In the short term, you could carry a lot of your team's workload on your shoulders, but that is not going to be sustainable. If you put everything on yourself, you will burn out sooner or later. Your team will not help you. They will not be happy because you took their jobs. They will be mad at you because you did not involve them or allow them to do what they are paid for. Nobody wants to feel useless.

You are only going to achieve results if you believe in teamwork. If you were a great individual achiever and were promoted because of that, that is okay. It is common, but as a manager, you need to change. You must stop being a solo player. Otherwise, you will fail. I was in category 1 and had always been a great employee. I worked well and performed.

When I became a manager, I saw how others were working. I felt like I could do everything better and faster. I started to handle a lot of the job by myself. I learned that it was not the right way. I had to change. I want to save you months of pain. I do not expect you to understand and change immediately. If you don't change quickly, that is normal. I am sure you will realize, sooner or later, what I am suggesting. When you feel too tired, like you are spending too many hours in the office, or working too often at home, you must realize you are working too much for yourself alone. Please notice it. Don't just think it will be better in the future. It will only be better if you start to believe in teamwork.

Your results depend on how involved you are with your team members. You have to understand that people are not like you. People don't think like you, people are not motivated by what motivates you, and people do not have the same goals as you. You need to adapt the way you manage to your team members. You must adjust your management style to each team member. It is difficult, but it is not impossible.

I assess people by looking at their strength in ideas and action. As a manager, you need to shorten the time between the idea and its action. You can draw a simple matrix to categorize your team members:

		Great Ideas but Low Action: "The Storyteller"	Great Ideas and Great Action: "The Star"
Idea (Think)	+		
		No Ideas and No Action: "The Walking Dead"	Low Ideas but Great Action: "The Executor"
	-	- Action (Do) +	

I suggest assessing your current team by following this framework. It will help you define how to manage your team members, and it will guide you toward the changes you need to make in the composition of your team. If you are building a new team, it will help you find the right profiles. The ideal strategy is to have as many stars as possible. Stars are people who generate a lot of ideas and have excellent action power. They make things happen. However, you are not going to have only stars on your team.

- Executors do not generate a lot of ideas, but they can make things happen. It is good to have executors. Ideas are important, but it is even more important to generate actions that bring those ideas to life. With no action, the idea is just a dream. Executors can help you a lot.
- Storytellers have ideas but no actions. My sales director introduced me to the business acronym of N.A.T.O.: No Action Talk Only. You need to be careful about this type of team member. Generating ideas is relatively easy. The hard part is generating good — or great — executable ideas and then execute. Someone on your team may generate great ideas, but not able to implement. You have to help that team member learn how to implement those ideas. Your job is to move this person to the next quadrant (the star). However, during the transition, you can ask the storyteller team member to work

with executors. Watch out for team members who do not generate good ideas. If they just throw out ideas that are not useful for the team, there is no value for you. If you cannot help the team member become more valuable, you have to get rid of him or her as soon as possible.

- The Walking Dead: There is no point in having someone on the team who does not contribute ideas nor actions. You need to get that person off the team immediately. The longer this person is on the team, the worse the effect will be on the team's dynamic. Why should other team members work hard if someone on the team does not add any value? You have a responsibility to let that person go. Do it quickly.

I would like to have as many stars as possible on my team. I need executors as well, but I will never have only executors. I also minimize the presence of storytellers, allowing only storytellers who have great ideas but still helping them to learn how to execute. On my ideal team, there is no space for the walking dead. My ideal team might not work in every business. You must find the right mix of team members depending on what is right for your situation. If you do not work on the right composition, you are not setting up the right conditions for success.

3.2 HOW TO PICK PEOPLE

In 2013, I was assigned to set up a subsidiary in Thailand. I interviewed many people and learned so much. I have been lucky enough to pick people and see if I made the right choice. I use a framework when I interview people. You can use it to assess your current team members.

A former team member asked me for some advice for questions to ask during a job interview. It is always a difficult decision since the interview is no longer than an hour or two. How can you have a meaningful interview? It is important to identify how the interviewee scores in the following areas:

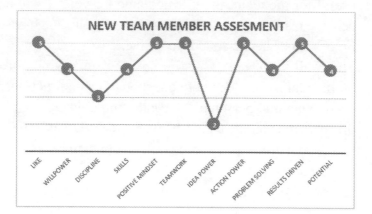

- like the job
- willpower
- discipline
- skillset
- positive attitude
- teamwork
- ideas generation
- action oriented
- problem solving
- results oriented
- potential

LIKE THE JOB: does the person like the job? Does the person want to continue in his current field? I have seen managers who do not consider this very much. If a person does not like the job, you cannot expect that the job will be done well. "Do you like this job? How much?." A compelling simple question.

WILLPOWER: is the person willing to put effort into the job? Is the person willing to put effort into succeeding? Is the person motivated to do a good job? I would like to have a fit body and a six-pack. Am

I willing to put in the effort? Not really. In a job, it is the same. If you like what you do but are not willing to put in the effort, you are not going to do a good job.

DISCIPLINE: is the person disciplined? If you want a fit body, you have to put in an effort at the gym and in your diet. Discipline means you can commit to a particular effort for a long time. An important proxy of discipline is time management. Time is a scarce resource. It is important to have people who respect deadlines. You cannot afford to have people who do not respect deadlines. Another aspect of discipline is being on time for meetings. Also, please note that different cultures in the world have different views about time. If time is important to you, you will need disciplined people. You need to avoid having undisciplined people on the team, regardless the country culture. If you have these people on your team, correct their behavior. You want people who deliver high-quality results on time.

SKILLSET: every job requires a different set of skills. During the interview, you have to understand if the candidate has the right skills. You can ask them to demonstrate certain skills. You can prepare case studies that are similar to the job the person is going to do. You will be able to assess the candidate much better if you have a deliverable to evaluate.

POSITIVE ATTITUDE: people behave and act based on their thoughts. I have worked with people who liked their jobs, put in the effort, and had the skills, but they were negative or pessimistic. I learned how important it is to hire positive people. When positive people are around you, positive energy will spread. They will find solutions, and they will not blame others. Positive people are happy and spread a good mood in the organization. I try to choose only positive people for my team. Try to avoid having negative people on your team. They will do the opposite of what positive people will do. They will not find solutions, and they will find someone to blame. Everything seems impossible to them. Their level of cooperation with

29

other team members will be poor. They will spread negative energy in the organization.

TEAMWORK: some people like to work with others, and some prefer to work alone. If you are a manager, you have to take care of team members who prefer to work alone. That is not necessarily a bad thing. However, avoid solo players who never sit down with other team members. I had a top performer who was smart and skilled. His problem was being individualistic. He was not able to work with others. He was not able to offer help to others and could not ask for help. In the end, he left my team, which was best for everyone. We hired a great team player, and the team dynamic improved already in the first week after he arrived.

IDEAS GENERATION: you want to understand if the future team member can generate ideas.

ACTION POWER: you want to understand if the future team member can make things happen.

PROBLEM SOLVING: in business, you will cope with problems. If you do not have problems to solve, it is bizarre. People react to challenges differently. Some people deal naturally with issues and find solutions. Others feel stress when solving problems. Some people are so overwhelmed that they do not perform at all and start making mistakes. On your team, you probably want to have people who want to solve issues, productively, managing well the pressure.

RESULTS ORIENTED: look for people who want to get results. In a best-case scenario, you will hire someone who finds pleasure in achieving goals. Achievers find joy in reaching goals. This is an excellent characteristic as you are measured on results. With more people who are results driven, your job is more straightforward. If you have people who are not interested in results, the results will not come.

POTENTIAL: try to assess a person's potential to handle more tasks and responsibilities. It can be challenging to evaluate this aspect in an interview. You will understand more when you work with the person, but it is good to have an initial assessment.

You can draw all these points in a graph and assess the candidate. If you decide to hire the person, you need to develop him or her in the weak areas.

This tool will help you structure an interview and assessment. However, do not blame yourself if you did not wholly understand the candidate during the interview. You will continuously assess your people and have chances to confirm or revise your assessments. You can make mistakes in an interview. If you apply a structured framework, you will reduce the chances of making a mistake. In interviews, always ask for examples of real-life experience.

3.3 HOW TO MANAGE PEOPLE

Managing people is a difficult job, but it can be enriching. Your results will depend upon others. The best way to manage people is to adapt your management style to the person you are managing. You cannot apply the same management style to everybody. A majority of managers have their management style and do not change it. That is wrong because you cannot ask others to adapt to you. Even if you are in a position of authority, you are not going to change the people around you. You do not control people. You can control yourself and consciously and intentionally adapt to others. Do not try to emulate authoritative bosses you might have seen in your experience. Those bosses will never get the best from their team members. If you want to be a great boss, adapt yourself to others.

I categorize team members based on four categories:

- **Motivation**
- **Skills**
- **Potential**
- **Discipline**

Motivation can be intrinsic or extrinsic. Some people are self-motivated and find the energy to go ahead within themselves (intrinsic motivation). Others are driven by external factors — like money (extrinsic motivation).

For skills, potential, and discipline, we can assign high or low values.

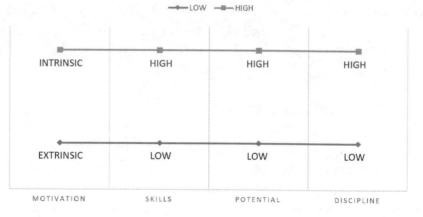

3.3.1 Type 1: The Great

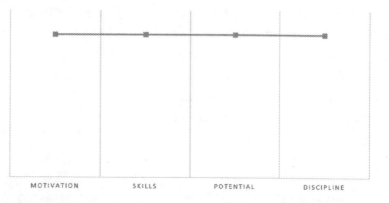

These exceptional team members have intrinsic motivation. You can count on them. They also have skills, potential (they will be ready for more responsibilities), and discipline (they deliver on time and with accuracy). If you have them, you are lucky. You can delegate any assignment to them. They have the potential to do more, and you can assign stretch goals. Your leadership style will be delegating. This team member will grow in the career path. You must help this person develop a good plan to move to the next level.

3.3.2 Type 2: The Poison

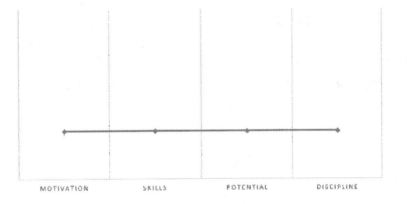

MOTIVATION   SKILLS   POTENTIAL   DISCIPLINE

They have extrinsic motivation, driven by money or materialistic rewards. They do not have skills, potential, or discipline. Get rid of these people quickly. The longer they stay in the organization, the more issues they will bring. It is your responsibility to let them go. Do not procrastinate. Do it immediately.

3.3.3 Type 3: The Great but Late

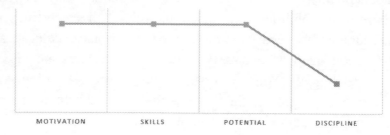

They have intrinsic motivation, good skills, and good potential — but they lack discipline. I was that kind of person. Even if I worked to improve my discipline, I still finished slightly late or got to meetings a bit late. If you manage this kind of person, you need to help them meet deadlines, show up to meetings on time, or be accurate on the job. Set clear deadlines and make sure they are respected. Coach the team member and help him/her understand how he/she can perform much better, just being more disciplined.

3.3.4 Type 4: The Solid Performer

They are driven by intrinsic motivation, have skills, and are disciplined, but they lack the potential for more responsibilities. They might lack the potential to move to the next level in the organization chart. Maybe they will never be ready to be the boss. That is okay. Not everybody wants to be the boss. You can count on their solid performance. You can delegate the job since they are experts. Just be careful about assigning tasks or responsibilities that are too stretched. You need to understand the limit and not cross it.

3.3.5 Type 5: The Baby Champion

They are driven by intrinsic motivation, do not have skills yet, but they have potential and discipline. Their issue is the lack of certain skills, but that is because probably they do not have much experience. Maybe they are still young. Your job is to develop them. You will assign direction, training, templates, and explain exactly how you want things to be done. You need to build their skills. Be clear about which skills are required — and structure a plan to build them. Be sure you have a clear timeline for the training plan. Treat it as a project. If you have the right raw material to work with, it is relatively easy to build skills. Once you are done, you have a star on your team.

3.3.6 Type 6: The Bonus Achiever

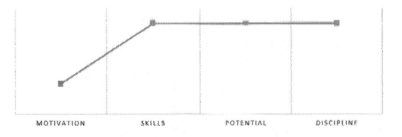

They are driven by extrinsic motivation; they have skills, potential, and discipline. They are motivated by external factors like money, promotion, or social recognition. Not everyone is self-motivated. Be careful since the motivation of this person can go up and down — depending on rewards. You need targets and incentives that are linked to performance. You have to manage the monetary part wisely to keep the motivation high. If your incentive and compensation systems are not appropriate, you will lose them. This kind of person will be attracted easily from job opportunities that will pay more than you do. You have to work on retention plans, so you need to evaluate if the level of effort to retain the person is worth. If they become too demanding, let them go. If you think it is worth, you could try to move the source of motivation from extrinsic to intrinsic. You have to coach a lot and offer a sense of purpose that is more meaningful than a materialistic reward. This is not easy and will not happen in the short term. If you can do it, you will have a star. You also have to work on punishments. It must be clear to the team member that if the team member performs will get rewards, but if performance is not achieved, then there are punishments. For example, in the case of low performance, a bonus is not paid. Remember to check the motivation level regularly. If you see a decrease in performance, it will not come back just by waiting. Take proper actions to work on the motivation of this team member.

3.3.7 Type 7: The Rich Baby

MOTIVATION   SKILLS   POTENTIAL   DISCIPLINE

They are driven by extrinsic motivation, do not have certain skills yet, but they have potential and discipline. Being motivated by external rewards, they might be eager to have salary increases. Money and bonuses could be important to them. You need to assign tasks that can be delivered with their current skills. You have to be direct and offer instructions and templates. You have to offer attractive packages and work on building skills. This person is an investment for you since you need to build skills. Skills are not developed overnight. However, do not be surprised if he/she leaves for another company who is offering better pay. For this reason, you need to be careful. You will have to decide if it makes sense and how much to invest.

3.3.8 Type 8: The Timer

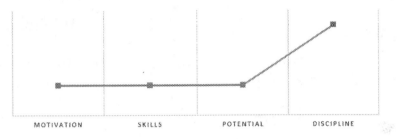

MOTIVATION   SKILLS   POTENTIAL   DISCIPLINE

They are driven by extrinsic motivation. They do not have skills, and they lack potential. They are disciplined. This is not a good team member. Assign them only what is possible to be delivered considering their lack of skills. Do not build any plan for the future since there is no potential there. The best you can get from this person is getting on-time assignments. They have extrinsic motivation, and they can quickly become unmotivated when rewards do not come. In the long run, due to the lack of skills and potential, they are not going to receive high bonuses or salary increases. Sooner or later, due to their lack of motivation, also discipline will decline. Try to find a replacement in the medium term.

3.3.9 Type 9: The Late Bonus Achiever

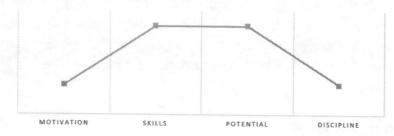

They are driven by extrinsic motivation; they have skills and potential but no discipline. You need to supervise them to meet deadlines or provide accurate work. You will also have to manage their motivation, as suggested for type 6 "the bonus achiever".

3.3.10 Type 10: The I Only Do This Late

They are driven by extrinsic motivation. They have skills, but they lack potential and discipline. The only good point is that they know how to do something. To get the best from them, supervise their deadlines and review the quality of their work. Those deadlines will be respected, and the job will be completed accurately. If you want to keep this person on your team, you need to teach them the importance of discipline. You can live without potential, but without discipline, you will be frustrated. You must improve the person's discipline. If they can finish the job on time — and deliver good quality without too much supervision — that is better than continuous supervision.

3.3.11 Type 11: The Late Rich Baby

MOTIVATION   SKILLS   POTENTIAL   DISCIPLINE

They are driven by extrinsic motivation. They do not have skills or discipline, but they have potential. This is probably a young team member with the potential to grow. They are not yet skilled and do not know how to be effective in time management. You have to teach them discipline, which requires a lot of short-term supervision, but it is an investment for the future. You have to decide how much effort you want to put in. You don't know how long it will take to build skills and discipline, so you need to be clear about how long you will give the person to live up to your expectations.

3.3.12 Type 12: The Bonus Solid Performer

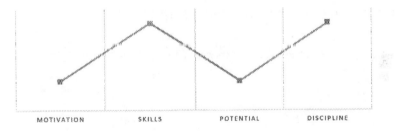

MOTIVATION   SKILLS   POTENTIAL   DISCIPLINE

They are driven by extrinsic motivation. They have skills and discipline, but they lack the potential to handle more responsibilities. Assign them tasks that are suitable for their skills and experience. They will perform. Do not assign instead stretched task. They will not deliver due to lack of potential. Materialistic rewards are important to them. Make sure they have the right incentives. You will need to manage their compensation.

3.3.13 Type 13: The Late Baby Champion

They are driven by intrinsic motivation. They do not have skills or discipline, but they have potential. This young team member has the potential to grow but does not know how to be effective in time management. You have to teach them discipline. This type requires a lot of short-term supervision, but it is an investment for the future. You have to decide how much effort you want to put in. It will not be sure that you will succeed. It is difficult to predict how long it will take to build skills and discipline. You need to be clear about how long you will give to the person to meet your expectations. Contrary to the "late rich baby", this person is self-motivated, and if you can win their heart and exploit their full potential, you will soon have a real talent on your team. Assign this person to work with a solid performer. Expose them to good role models.

3.3.14 Type 14: The I Would Like but I Can't Now

They are driven by intrinsic motivation. They do not have skills, discipline, and potential. This person would like to do a good job but is not able to due to lack of skills, potential, and discipline. They are willing to work long hours, but nothing gets done. You will be confused when you see the person working hard, but sooner or later, you will realize that nothing happens. This person is willing to work hard. You can coach the person and develop their skills and discipline. The person is self-motivated, and a good conversation about their development plan can help. It is important for the person to be aware of the issues. Work first on discipline and then skills. There is no point to work on potential before discipline and skills are set. If they do not improve, you need them to leave.

3.3.15 Type 15: The Late Performer

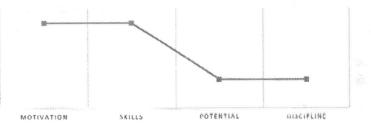

They are driven by intrinsic motivation. They have skills, but they are not disciplined. They lack the potential for more responsibilities. They must learn first to respect deadlines and deliver on time, so focus on teaching them discipline. Coaching sessions can be beneficial. If the development plan is successful, you got a new solid performer in your team.

3.3.16 Type 16: The I Would Like to but I Can't

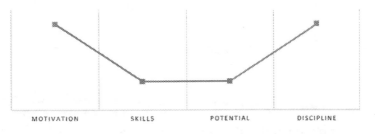

They are driven by intrinsic motivation. They do not have skills and potential. They have discipline. There are no issues with timing or accuracy. You can work on a step-by-step skills-development plan. Assign them only what is possible and gradually increase their responsibilities as their skills grow. Have a clear skills-development plan — and assign them to work with a solid performer — and you will have another solid performer on the team. It is a good investment.

3.4 DELEGATION AND ACCOUNTABILITY

A manager will only succeed with the cooperation of their team members. You have to adapt your management style to the different employee types on your team. You also have to make a lot of efforts to learn how to manage yourself.

Once you picked the right people for your team, carefully assessed them, and know how to manage them, you still must complete two additional steps:

- delegating the right job to the right people
- keeping your people accountable

3.4.1 Delegating

You picked the right people, assessed them, and now your company is paying their salaries and bonuses. Now, you need to delegate tasks and responsibilities. As a new manager, you might find difficult to assign jobs to others. Before, you were doing the job by yourself and did not have to assign it to anyone else. It is a new situation for you, and you might not be familiar with delegation. Learning how to delegate effectively as fast as possible is a must for a manager.

At the beginning of my career, I was doing jobs that should have been done by someone else. I found it difficult to ask others. I was not used to having subordinates. Before, I only had colleagues and bosses. Once I became the boss, I had to tell others what to do. If you are in the same situation, you must learn how to delegate effectively:

- Follow the course of action suggested in this book (start with a vision, priority settings, and action plans).
- Pick the right people and assess them.
- Decide what aspects you need to adapt of yourself to manage the specific team member.
- Assign priorities and actions to the right layer in your organization.
- Set deadlines for the team or person.
- Set and share the quality standards you expect.
- Confirm that the person or team understands what has been assigned. They must understand the deadline and agree to all aspects of the assignment. If they do not agree, you need to clarify all the elements and get an agreement. Otherwise, you did not delegate effectively and will be disappointed by the results. It is better to have a meaningful and constructive discussion than to discover that you are not happy with the results.
- Follow the personality types to define your management style.
- If the task or project is not completed on time or with the quality you want, check what went wrong and restart from there.

Delegating is a never-ending activity. You will delegate every single day. You will become better and better. It is just a matter of practice. This framework can help you speed up the process. When you become competent at delegating, you will be a better manager.

A graph can help you understand how to adapt your management style to the different kinds of people on your team. You cannot have only one management style. You are one, but the people you manage are many. You need to be able to play several management styles. You must be a people manager and learn how to adapt to others. Look at the characteristics of your team members (skills, potential, discipline, motivation). Identify in which maturity stage they are in.

Maturity, in this case, is not about age. It is about the level the person achieved in the four characteristics. A mature team member is high in all four categories. A terrible team member scores low in all four. You will delegate, praise, and encourage fully mature team members. On the contrary, you will give very detailed instructions and supervision to the terrible ones.

Follow the "Do line" to manage in the right way. Do not follow the "Don't line". I hope this graph is easy to read. It is common sense, but many managers do not apply it in practice.

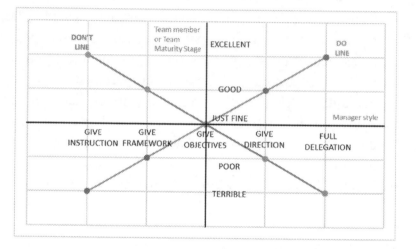

The agility to move from one management style to another is one of the most difficult things to do because it requires changing yourself (depending on the person you are speaking to). This applies to team members and entire teams as well. For example, if you are the general manager, you will have teams with different maturity levels. The way you manage your teams will change.

The two lines, do and don't, cross in the "just fine" maturity stage. This is the most difficult stage as it requires to combine several aspects. Here giving just objectives is not enough; it will require to move on the right and left of the axis, offering encouragement, but also more guidelines and framework when required. If you manage well, those people, or teams, will move in a better maturity stage, becoming better professionals or better teams.

3.4.2 Accountability

Accountability is the second part of the delegation process. When you delegate something, you expect the team or person to deliver. Accountability is a sign of respect for the job done by others. If you followed all the right steps of the delegation process, your people would be accountable. When you do not get what has been agreed, you need to have a feedback session with the team member. If you find the cause of the poor delivery, do not be timid. You can take corrective action.

When your team does a poor job, you need to question yourself as well. Do not think your team member is the only one responsible. A poor job means you did not do everything you could have done. There is no case where you are not responsible — even when you are working with someone who has extrinsic motivation, no skills, no potential, and no discipline. You are still responsible because you decided to keep that team member on your team.

3.5 REWARDING YOUR TEAM

If you picked the right people and are managing them well, you will get results. Teamwork and the right people are the keys to success. You do not succeed alone. They do not succeed without you. Everyone needs everyone else. When the team wins, it is important to reward the effort and results. Be sure to recognize and acknowledge people.

Rewards can be split into rational-emotional and tangible-intangible:

- A rational reward is something an employee can see, listen, or touch. Imagine a salary increase after a good year. The employee will see the rise in the new paycheck. Imagine a promotion with a new job title that will be seen on a business card. Imagine a career plan or a special bonus.

- Emotional rewards are something employees can feel. Imagine a recognition speech in front of others, a thank-you note, or a special project or assignment. When you give emotional rewards, employees feel proud, appreciated, recognized, and important.

Rewards can be tangible, if materialistic, or intangible, if not physical.

NATURE OF REWARD	TANGIBLE	• Special gift/surprise • Credit in front of others • Talk good to others • Written Thank you note	• Salary Increase • Bonus • Performance review form • Business review with Top Management
	INTANGIBLE	• Trust • Encouragement • Support • Recognition 1on1 • Acknowledgment 1on1 • Thank you 1on1	• Job Title • Career path • Feedback on performance • Participation to goal settings
		EMOTIONAL	RATIONAL
		TYPE OF REWARD	

To manage well, you need to decide on proper rewards. Tangible rewards help boost morale in the short term. Intangible rewards help more in the long term, and they build a sense of belonging and loyalty. A balance between the four types will help keeping employees engaged and loyal in the short term and the long term. If you only use one type of reward, it will be less effective over time. For example, if you continuously praise your team members in front of others for everything they do, but when it comes to the salary increase for the new year, why would you not offer an increase? Do you think your frequent public praise will continue to help morale? What if you increase people's salaries every year, but you never say thank you or praise them in front of others. Do you think people will be genuinely engaged with you?

Another key aspect is the timing of the reward. The general principle is simple: if it is genuine, every moment is okay. Authenticity is important. If you fake the reward to get a short-term boost, people will feel it. If you believe a team member deserves a reward for a special contribution, that is the right time.

3.5.1 Common Rewards and Timelines

Salary increases. There are usually certain times and processes to follow. You need to focus on the salary increase you are offering. You need to assess and decide what salary increase to offer. You cannot just do it as the last thing of the day or delegate it only to HR. The new salary will stay with your team member for at least the following twelve months. You cannot make mistakes. An increase of 2–3 percent makes a difference. It is easy to make a mistake when you manage many employees, and salary increases are calculated in a cold spreadsheet. That number is how you reward your team members for the jobs they have done.

The same goes for yearly bonuses. You need to focus and make sure everybody gets a fair bonus, reflecting the real performance and results achieved. If the calculation is delegated to HR or the Finance Department, you need to confirm your people are getting what they deserve. If the calculation is not fair, you must fight for them.

At least once a year, you will have a performance review with your people. It is a critical moment. You and your team member reflect on what has been done. You can address issues, but it is vital to say what has been done well. If you put the performance review in a written format, it becomes a tangible reward.

With promotions, it is time to celebrate the team member's achievement. There will be a new job title and a new work phase. It is a unique moment to praise team members and wish them good luck in the future. When a team member has done well and is ready for a promotion, you need to help them get it. You are the boss, and you can make sure your people are in the pipeline for promotions. Help your people improve their careers. They will remember that you helped them.

Provide feedback immediately after a good performance. When you see a great performance, do not wait until the yearly performance review to say something. Go to that team member and tell them what you liked. You can reward good behaviors every time you see them. This will help people understand what you appreciate. What they should do will be clearer to them. When you give positive feedback, you make clear that they have done well. If you do not provide feedback, they will be in doubt. With positive feedback, you can build confidence. The critical point is authenticity. If you praise just for the sake of it, you will just add confusion. People will not understand why you appreciated them. They will think you just paid them lip service.

Team gatherings, town hall meetings, quarterly reviews, or yearly kickoffs are good times to publicly recognize special contributions.

For special contributors, you might decide to issue a special bonus or gift. It could be a good idea to give a written thank-you note to the team member. Receiving a special bonus is good for the bank account, but saying thank you is good for the soul.

When you are in meetings, having coffees, or eating lunch, you can always say something good about someone who did a good job. When you talk positively about somebody, you are improving their reputation.

Give credit to others. You are the manager and do not exist without your team. If they do not work well, you achieve nothing. Your success comes if they succeed. A positive result is the result of their work. You should always give credit to your team and expose them to top management. Give them credit and visibility. Let top management know who your people are. Tell them what they are doing and what they have achieved.

Trust people. People know if you trust them or not. If you do not trust them, tell them why. Tell them what they need to improve. Trust is not given for free. If you trust someone who did not earn it, you are a naïve manager. You are not Pollyanna, but if a team member can be entrusted with a task or a project, let them feel trusted. When you trust people who can be trusted, you will get great performance. If you distrust people who can be trusted, you will never win over people's hearts. They will never respect you.

You will be a good manager if you believe in others and are altruistic. If you are selfish and egocentric, you are not going to be good at rewarding people. You could be good with tangible and rational rewards. Those are the easy ones that even selfish managers can apply. Other rewards require empathy and putting others before you.

3.6 IT'S TIME FOR ACTION

Have you assessed your team members? Which type are they? Reflect on your management style.

- Are you adapting your management style to the maturity stages of your team members?
- Are you applying the same management style to everyone?
- If you are applying the same management style, how can you start managing better?
- What benefits do you see for yourself and others if you start managing differently, adapting yourself to others?

4

TRACKING

To run a modern business, you must have measurements. Do you agree? Only what you measure gets done. Measuring is a critical part of your job as a manager. Your role is not the closest to action. Your team members are closer to the field, where things happen. Your role is to define the purpose, goals, priorities, action plans, and reviews.

You work a lot on planning for the future, but you need to spend even more time measuring progress. Measuring, or tracking, must be a central part of your daily routine. You have to define the best reporting to help you understand if the organization is moving in the right direction — and right speed — toward the goals. Without good reporting, you will be blind. Your success will be in the hand of Lady Luck. You want to be in control of events as much as possible. There will always be something outside your control, but try to measure as many aspects of your business as possible. Start from tracking the key parts of your business, and after the key areas are under control, you can move to the ones less important.

4.1 REPORTING

Reporting is not just a piece of paper or an electronic document that you receive, look at, and throw away. A good report will give to you and your team key information critical for the job. If a report is not providing valuable information, it is better not to have it. That useless report is wasting the time of the people who are preparing and reading it. Most of all, useless report risks giving the wrong information, that can drive your organization to take the wrong actions. You need to make sure your organization is using the right reporting.

You have to decide on the frequency of reports. You will have reports issued daily, weekly, monthly, quarterly, and yearly. You have to ask yourself which frequency is most meaningful. The answer is not as frequently as possible for every report. IT capabilities are so powerful that — with the right hardware and software — you could bombard your organization with tons of daily data. The more reporting you introduce, the more you are asking your people to spend time reading and digesting the information. It can be a big distraction. You must be sure your people receive the right information at the right time.

Another part of reporting is defining the right template. With poor reporting, information is presented in a way that requires a long time to understand. A report must give readers information that triggers an immediate corrective action. A report that requires effort to read is ineffective.

Do not think that defining the report is someone else's job. Do not think you define the strategy, and others take care of reports. That is not a good approach. Make sure your people are reading the right information at the right time and spending as little time as possible to understand it. The proper format will make you feel more secure and avoid misunderstandings.

Consider where the report is available. Reports are sent by email, stored in common folders, or stored in folders that are not accessible for everyone. Once you have the report, it must be accessible in an easy way. The information must be easily available. Sometimes the way the report is delivered is wrong. If important reports are stored in the wrong place, only a few people will open them. Some reports take up gigabytes of space. People will be annoyed if they have to remove continuously large reports from their inboxes, and they are not going to open the files.

Keep in mind the following points:

- Why does the report exist?
- Who will receive the report?
- What is the objective of the report?
- When will the report be issued? How frequently?
- How will the report look? Is the report easy to read?
- How will it be stored or sent? By email? In a common folder?

The following matrix will help you understand if everything is good or if you need to adjust something.

Dept.	Report Name	Objective	For Who?	Frequency	Format	Where is it stored?	Is the Report Meaningful?	Corrections Required
Sales	a							
	b							
	c							
....								

Once the reports are set and you are happy with all the points above, it is time to make it real. If you notice the person who is responsible for preparing the report is not working effectively, you have to intervene. Reporting drives your business. Do not consider reporting a secondary priority — or not a priority at all. That is a common mistake for managers. Many managers delegate this activity to business analysts or the Finance Department. Delegating is okay, but delegating is not neglecting. If you decide to delegate the reporting, you need to make sure the right job gets done.

Reporting is run typically by analytical people. You always need to consider this as an alert. Analytical people are very good with numbers, but they tend to complicate reporting. They are comfortable with spreadsheets, formulas, and KPIs, but few people in the organization will be able to understand. Even if someone can read the reports, they are spending a considerable amount of time reading them. This is not efficient. You need to make sure the average person can read the reports. You need to make sure the receiver can get valuable information in the blink of an eye. If you have very analytical people preparing reports, you need to make sure the readability of the report is ok.

When you have people dedicated to reporting, you may have too many reports. Some managers abuse tracking too. Your business will not grow just having one more useless report. Do not fall in the trap of thinking a report means everything is under control. Be wise, be careful, and look at the reporting in your organization. If you are not happy, revise it as soon as possible.

What reporting do you want to see for yourself? When do you want to see it? How does the report look? Who will prepare it? You need to take care of the needs of your organization, but you also need to take care of yourself. You need reporting to do your job — but do not abuse the reports for yourself. Do not abuse your authority by ordering useless reports. You must be a role model for your people. Ask for the right reports at the right time. Everything starts with you. Your organization will mirror you.

4.2 MEETINGS: TIMING AND TYPES

Another form of tracking is meetings. When I started as a manager, I did not have any clue about when I should meet my team, when I should meet the whole organization, and when I should meet individuals. This is a common problem for new managers. You will become good — it is a matter of practice and finding your way. There is no universal rule to define when meetings should happen. It depends a lot on the preferences and needs of you and your team.

First, there are meetings with individuals, departments, multiple departments, and the entire company.

Second, meetings will be about updating a situation, aligning plans, planning future actions, tracking progress, discussing issues, and finding solutions.

In my experience, the key meetings are:

- whole organization meeting at the beginning of the year
- whole organization quarterly meetings
- quarterly or monthly leadership team meetings (your direct reports)
- department quarterly or monthly meetings
- 1on1 meetings

The whole organization must gather at the beginning of the year for the yearly plan. This will help you keep everybody on the same page. People want to know what the company will do. They want to know about forecasts (if the company expects to do well or not). This is a good time for managers to reinforce the vision, goals, and priorities. It will help reinforce a sense of unity toward a common goal.

Quarterly meetings with the whole organization will update the progress on the business and next programs. It is great to celebrate successes together. It will reinforce a sense of unity and trust for the future.

In quarterly leadership meetings, the team is the management line. You need to have at least one meeting every quarter with your leadership team.

It is good to have a department meeting every month. It can align performance and plans.

Depending on the maturity of your management team, you can consider having a monthly meeting with them. If your management team is new and does not have alignment yet, it is better to do it.

Some departments need to meet every week. I have a sales meeting every week to control the current and expected performance for the month and quarter.

Meet with your team members weekly, biweekly, monthly, or quarterly. It depends on your need and your team member's need. If all is good, a quarterly one-on-one meeting is probably enough. If you are not happy yet with the results, consider a weekly one-on-one meeting.

As for reporting, you need to decide why, when, where, what, how, and who participates. Too many meetings can take up a lot of extra time. If you decide to have a meeting, wonder if you can achieve the same goal without the meeting. The fewer meetings you have, the more time your people have to work. You are the manager, and you have to decide how your people spend their time. If you see too many meetings, please ask yourself if they are all required.

dept./ people	meeting name	Objective	Attendees	frequency and when	deliverable	where	Is the meeting meaningful?	Corrections required
whole company								
Sales	a							
	b							
	c							

- Why does the meeting exist? Is there a meaning? If not, you do not need it.
- Who will participate?
- What is the objective of the meeting?
- When will the meeting be done?
- Which deliverables will be discussed? Excel files? PowerPoint? Conversations?
- Where will the meeting take place? In the office? Off-site location? At a desk or in a meeting room?

Who should attend the meeting? You only need to have people who can add value. Meetings with too many attendees are not successful because no one feels responsible for being there. Be clear on who you want to attend the meeting. Unnecessary people are better left out. What is the objective? You need to be crystal clear. You need to know what outcome you are looking for. It is great to build a routine for meetings. Schedule them for the same day at the same hour with the same agenda.

Which deliverables will be discussed? How will the outcome of the meeting be recorded? Effective meetings must have a standard format. In my weekly sales meetings, we always look at the same report for past sales and the same form for forecasting. Using the same form every time builds a routine and makes meetings faster. If the meeting is a conversation, it is important to follow a template and record what has been said. You are responsible for making the meeting productive. Usually, I prepare a few slides to drive the conversation. If you list the topics you want to discuss, it will help the team.

Keeping minutes is another key element of a successful meeting. That will help you record the next actions and deadlines. It is precious. At the beginning of my career, I was going to meetings without templates and not keeping minutes. The meetings were taking forever and had no real conclusion. Even after a good meeting, the content was disappearing after a few hours or days. Always identify clear deliverables. The meeting must conclude with a summary of the discussion and a list of decisions taken and next steps. It is important to have clear deadlines for the next steps and highlight who is responsible. The minutes of the meeting will have those elements. Share the minutes from the meeting with all attendees within a couple of days.

Where will the meeting take place? Recurring meetings should take place in the same space. Identify a meeting room and use the same for the same meeting. That will help build a routine, and the meeting will become more effective. People will be comfortable and will not be distracted by new places.

Use off-site meetings for quarterly or yearly meetings, budget allowing. People will have more energy and feel refreshed. The meetings will run smoothly, and people will feel excited. With virtual teams, it is important to have a fast, stable connection — preferably with video. With an excellent internet connection and software, you can replicate a lot of the physical world.

Even though we are all adults, there can be distractions in meetings: funny ringtones, online chats, WhatsApp messages, phone calls, and email notifications. You want to have a productive meeting, and distractions are not good for that. You must be clear about the rules of the meeting. It is better to set the rules at the beginning of the meeting than to continuously stop because of distractions. Be clear with your people.

In the beginning, I felt uncomfortable telling people I was annoyed by distractions. I thought I should not have to teach people basic civil rules. I was wrong. On a PowerPoint slide, you can list the basic behaviors you want people to follow.

Do's

- Always express your opinion. There are no stupid ideas.
- Ask the speakers to repeat a topic if you do not understand what they are saying. If you did not understand, others probably did not either.
- Respect others' opinions. You can politely disagree.
- Switch off all your devices.
- Stay present. Give your contribution. You are there to participate actively.
- If there is something urgent that requires you to leave, inform the manager at the beginning.
- If you are not interested, you can leave the room.

Don'ts

- Do not keep your computer open.
- Do not send or read emails.
- Do not check on your mobile phone.
- Do not be distracted.
- Do not be there if you are not interested.

You might feel strange doing this. If you don't want to waste time, prepare your list for your next meeting. Try to build a routine. If you enforce those rules at the beginning, it will become a habit for your team. Do it as soon as possible. Do not let bad habits get in your way.

Always ask yourself why the meeting exists. Do not schedule unnecessary meetings. You do not want to waste yours and people's time. Remember that time is against you. You cannot waste it.
You will identify the need for meetings in your organization. You need to be disciplined. Who do you need to meet? When? How frequently? What do you want to discuss? Be disciplined for yourself. Do not call meetings to just have superficial conversations about a generic topic with no specific agenda or goal. Avoid ad hoc meetings as much as possible. You are in a position of authority and can call meetings of your subordinates, but you cannot abuse your authority. Do not call useless meetings. If you do, you cannot expect the meetings to be productive. Act as a role model. Everything starts with you. Your organization mirrors you.

4.3 DEBRIEFING

I started using debriefings after business reviews with our top management. When the boss visited our office, usually for a quarterly review or a market visit, I started a debriefing immediately after he left. I asked the team members how they felt during the visit. I found a formula that combined the qualitative and descriptive parts of a normal debriefing, and I added a quantitative part to get a score. I have a debriefing after the team is involved in a particular performance: meeting with customers, meeting with top management, important internal meetings. I want to understand how the team members felt. This is about feelings and emotions. Feeling ready or not ready is subjective. If you decide to try this type of debriefing, you will probably see how different people perceive the same events. Ask your team members to list all the items in the three categories as shown in the table below and assign a score from one to ten about their feelings. If they felt extremely ready, they would put a ten. For the other two categories, they could put a ten to signal their total unreadiness. When you collect the items, the score will help you debrief them objectively. Allocate some time for self-reflection, and it can be shared in public afterward. Collect the data in a spreadsheet so that you can analyze the results. You will have a template for each team member:

I felt ready on		I was not ready on (but I should have been)		I was not ready on (but it was never discussed before)	
Item	Score (1–10)	Item	Score (1–10)	Item	Score (1–10)
A		D		G	
B		E		H	
C		F		I	
Total (X)		Total (Y)		Total (Z)	

At this point, you have an incredible amount of qualitative and quantitative data.

You can see all the items listed in meaningful categories. Knowing that a person felt ready is important. Sometimes you will be surprised to see that someone felt ready, but you thought the opposite. You and your team member perceive a different reality. On the contrary, you will discover that someone did not list a point that according to you, they did very well. You want to build confidence on your team, and it helps if you can highlight what the team member did well but did not notice. The same is valid for the other two categories. What scores did they assign? Did they see the same reality as you?

The scores will give you a perspective of the overall team. Did the team score high in the "ready" category? That is great. Did they score high in the "not ready but I should be" category? That is bad. You want the team to be ready. Did they score high in "not ready but it was never discussed" category? That is less dramatic since people cannot blame themselves for not being ready for topics that were never discussed before. If there are a lot of items and high scores in this category, you need to question why. If too many topics were new or were not properly introduced, people may have felt very uncomfortable, and this does not help high performance.

You can see the net scores:

- X-Y will give you the "net first score," which is the total score of what the team felt ready for (minus what they did not feel ready for but should have). You want to be in a positive sign. The higher the score, the better your team felt.
- X-Y-Z will give you the "net second score," which is deducting the scores of the third category. The ideal score is a positive sign. It will be less than the net first score, but do not consider the last category a big alert. It is good to see the net second score — but focus first on the first one.
- You can do net scoring by person. You will understand how individuals felt. This will give you a clear direction if you are aligned with their reality. If you did not feel a good performance, but your team member put those items in the "ready" category or did not list the items at all, you need to have a feedback session.

If you are disciplined and make this debriefing a habit, you will see a trend. How was the team feeling a year ago, six months ago, three months ago, and now? What will you do to help your team members to feel more prepared in the future? You are part of the team, and you need to take the same exercise with them. You also need to close the debrief session with a summary of your key comments: share what you think was good, celebrate and recognize the team, but also be clear about what you are not satisfied with.

4.4 IT'S TIME FOR ACTION

Assess your reporting:

- Which reports do you regularly use?
- Is your reporting effective and efficient? Is it useful?
- Do you have redundant reports?
- Is it easy to read the reports?

Assess your meetings:

- Which meetings do you regularly have?
- Are your meetings effective and efficient? Are they useful?
- Do you have redundant meetings?

How do you debrief with your team? Do you have a regular practice of debriefing? Is your team learning from past experiences?

5

KEEPING THE WHOLE IN BALANCE

Business is a balancing act. Any imbalance will affect your performance negatively. The more you balance the whole, the better you perform. Business results depend on many factors. One of the tasks you are required to complete is keeping the whole in balance. Before becoming a manager, you had to complete tasks. You were focused on a piece of the whole. That task was part of a bigger project, that project was part of a bigger goal, and that goal was part of a bigger vision. Now that you are a manager, you have to manage the whole.

5.1 THE BUSINESS CIRCLE

I defined eight main parts you will need to keep in balance. If you can score good or great results in each area, your business will most likely be successful. If some areas score low, you will suffer in those areas. You will have some negative effects, but if you score low in too many areas, your business most likely will fail or at least strongly suffer.

The eight areas are listed in order of priority:

- **Goals**
- **Organization**
- **Motivation**
- **Processes**
- **Systems**
- **Discipline**
- **Execution**
- **Innovation**

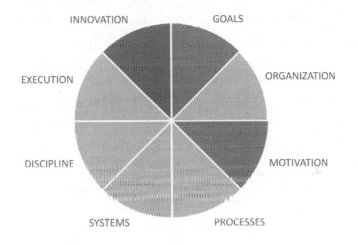

Goals: your team must be clear. If the direction is not clear, how can you expect the team to achieve? You need to be sure the destination is clarified for all team members.

Organization: has the organization the right set up? Are all the required departments present? Once the goal is set, there can be a lack of thinking about the best way to organize the teams. Some departments could be missed entirely. Are all the right people in the right places? Do you have a good organization chart? Do you have the right people in place? Are your departments optimized? Do you have enough people? A business without the right people or the right number of people is not going far. You might have goals all set and clear, but if the organization is not sustaining those goals, they are just visions and dreams.

Motivation: you need to have engaged and committed people to deliver. You have to check regularly the motivation level of your people. You can assess all your interactions with people, and you have to do it with your observation. I always scan the motivation and moods of the people around me. You have to work intentionally on motivating people. This is a difficult part of your job, and it requires IQ and EQ.

Processes: you need to ensure departments and people have smooth, simple, fast processes to communicate and work, internally and externally. You cannot imagine how much time is lost in poor processes. There is always a way to improve the way that your team is working. There will always be a way to make things faster and better. A majority of people are reluctant to take the initiative and challenge the status quo. The inefficient and ineffective processes will exist until someone reengineers them. Do not underestimate how much time and confusion exists on your team. You need to detail the process to understand what is happening. You have to come up with a better way. Everything starts with you. If you start to improve your processes, your team will absorb it into its culture. If you do not care, they will not care. There are many simple, accessible, and inexpensive technologies to facilitate teams to interact. Cloud applications can store files, QR/bar code readers can help you to scan a massive number of items, and popular conference tools like Skype help to communicate very easily. Some applications, like Microsoft PowerBI, help to manage an incredible quantity of data. Technology is one part of improving processes. The other part is simplifying the decision-making process. How do you make sure the process allows people to know if a decision is required? I had customers who had issues with their payments. Should I sell to customers who did not pay their bills on time? Should I sell to customers who had not paid bills in the past? This must be a careful decision. It must also be made quickly. In the beginning, I had a process that was taking too long from request to decision. An email would ask if I would approve a credit to a customer. There were no details in that email, and I had to ask for more information about the credit situation of that customer. I would receive an email with the details in an Excel file that was not standardized. Every time, I had to look somewhere else for the information I needed to decide. There was a long trail of emails that asked for confirmation or new explanations. The request email sent to me had a generic subject line that did not communicate the urgency, and I was not able to take care of the issue as soon as possible, simply because I did not understand how urgent the request was. We were taking too long, and everybody was frustrated. In the end, we were always late. I decided to review the process. The emails needed a standard subject line: "Urgent — Approve Credit, Customer Name." This helped me identify the urgency. In the body of the email, a standard table showed current bills and amount of credit to approve. In the last column, the credit controller suggested releasing or not the credit. A standard spreadsheet was attached.

The new process was much more effective. I could quickly identify the issue. I had all the information I needed to decide. I had a suggestion about releasing or not. If I needed more information, I had an Excel file with additional information. We dramatically cut down the number of emails, and 99 percent of requests could be approved within thirty minutes. Every request was approved or rejected the same day. I felt in control of the process. I always made an informed decision. The credit controller could complete the task quickly, avoiding double work. Taking care of the processes will improve your ability to make decisions.

Systems: with the current technologies, we are full of powerful IT systems. Big companies invest in expensive systems. Smaller companies can have good systems, as well. They can maximize the capabilities of spreadsheets and database tools. However, costly systems do not necessarily mean sound systems. In my organization, everybody was complaining about the complexity, the slow speed, and the lack of user manuals. In the end, we had an expensive system that few people understood how to use.

Sometimes, you do not have a system at all. I was managing part of a sales force that still took orders on paper! That is not the best way to get sales orders and guarantee fast and accurate delivery to customers. It takes time to upload the order, and there are sometimes mistakes because of handwriting is not clear enough. You need to help your people work with a good system. This is a difficult part of your job. In big companies, only IT is entitled to change the system. If you cannot change or upgrade your systems, you can always try to improve the ability of your people, for example, making sure regular trainings are organized and user manuals are available.

Discipline: this is the ability of an organization to work on time and with accuracy. You want to have an organization that can work within a timeline. You might have worked on the previous five aspects, but if you do not keep the organization accountable to deliver on time and with quality, you are not maximizing the job you have already done.

Execution: the ability to execute will depend largely on the six earlier topics. If you have done a great job with them, your organization is probably executing well. However, there may be circumstances that are out of your control. A third-party agency may not be doing the job properly. A customer might have a different interest that does not allow you to work effectively or efficiently. Your headquarters might have new guidelines. There is always something you cannot fully control. Try to anticipate and manage as much as possible those circumstances.

Innovation: you must always think about how to innovate the way you and your organization work. Look at goals, organization, motivation, processes, systems, discipline, and execution. There are always new ways of doing things. Do not be satisfied with the status quo. Always improve.

It is important to assess your status for each element. Ask all your team members for their assessment. They can use simple colors:

- Red is not okay.
- Orange is not so good — but not bad.
- Green is okay.

In October 2015, I made a business circle about my business unit. The circle can be utilized in any department. If applied to the Sales Department, how will it look? What about your other departments? Ask your department heads and team members to assess their department. Are the managers and team members aligned? Do they see the same picture? What are the key areas to work on? The key to a successful action plan is to have green in all eight slices.

I asked all employees to color in their assessments. After one year, there were more greens and fewer reds. The red areas were in systems where we did not have a lot of power to intervene. My assessment was close to the one given by employees. The employees had a red area, and it was orange for me. That gave me a clear direction.

For a large organization with a lot of employees, it will not be possible to have the business circle colored directly by employees. You could launch an internal survey to get scores and then color the slices based on the scores. You need to find a way to assess your current situation, and you need an action plan with a clear timeline and responsibilities. Do not neglect the green areas. They are green today, but that does not mean it will remain at that level. Efforts are required to maintain green areas in the future. The eight points are listed in order of priority. The first areas to work on are those that show red in the first positions. The worst case is if you have a red area for goals. You need to correct it immediately and make it green as fast as possible. Once you have identified gaps and decided on an action plan, you need to follow up. Do not just do the exercise and then keep things as they are. Act. Take decisions. Make things happen. Change your reality. You can do it. If you do not start, nobody else will do it for you. Fill a simple matrix with your action plan and review it regularly, monthly and quarterly (see chapter 10.4).

5.2 THE BUSINESS TRIANGLE

In your management role, you have to work hard to balance your organization. Keeping the whole in perfect equilibrium is difficult. You need to have at least good equilibrium; perfection may be too ambitious. You will probably be working with scarce resources and need to achieve high objectives. This is the basis of capitalism. In a for-profit organization, you are there to make profits by maximizing revenues and minimizing costs. Managers have to be able to work constantly to maximize results and minimize resources. As a manager, do not complain about having to deliver more with the same or fewer resources! Capitalism is not changing to a new paradigm to minimize profits. If one day, the manager can work to reduce output (results) and increase input (resources), then or the company is going bankrupt, or the company is not working on Earth.

You are required to balance three main elements:

- **Expectations**: what results does your company expect from your department or business unit?
- **People**: do you have the right people and the right number of people to achieve those results?
- **Systems and Processes**: do you have systems and processes in place to help your people achieve the expected results?

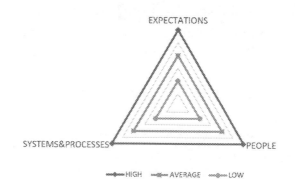

You need to work to keep those three elements in equilibrium. You can visualize the equilibrium as an equilateral triangle. In an ideal world, you would have high expectations, the right number, and quality of people, and the right systems and processes. This is the ideal you are trying to achieve. However, the whole will still be in balance if you want to achieve average expectations and equip your organization with an average number and quality of people — with average systems and processes. You also have balance if expectations, people, systems, and processes are all poor. Most likely, in any situation, you will have not an equilateral triangle. This is why you are required to find a balance between the three elements.

My company had high expectations, but we were working with lean organizations and so few people. We sometimes did not have qualitative systems and processes in place. Managers and employees were in a constant struggle to hit targets. They were constantly coping with systems and processes that did not help. In this situation, it was normal to lose people who look for more balanced companies.

If you are in a similar situation, you have to work to improve your processes and systems. You need to have as much efficiency as possible to compensate for the low number of people. You have to work to keep the right people in the organization because the few that you have must deliver.

You have to develop continuously and constantly motivate your people. You have to work with your company to set the right expectations as well. You need to manage up. You cannot just agree with every stretch goal assigned from the top. You have to make sure they compromise by lowering expectations or equip you with more and better resources.

Using the triangle, you can have three main situations:

- **Wishful Thinking**: high expectations but not enough good people, systems, or processes.
- **Government Office**: low in expectations, systems, and processes. High in people.

- **Switched off High-Processor PC**: low in expectations and people but high in systems and processes.

If you are in the Wishful Thinking situation, you have a tough job rebalancing your situation. You need to achieve a lot without the right resources. You need to get your management to agree to adjust expectations to your reality and in the meanwhile, to improve your systems, processes, and people. I have also seen managers exacerbate their situations. Many managers overcommit on stretch goals to be seen as aggressive managers who are willing to overachieve. Overexcitement is a positive characteristic, but it is not what must be done when the resources are too limited. In this case, the objective is a good balance.

WISHFUL THINKING TRIANGLE

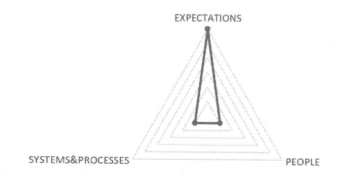

The Government Office situation is more typical in public offices than private companies. If you are in this situation, you are not maximizing your outcomes. If you are lucky enough to have the right number of people and the right quality, you can put them to use by increasing expectations and improving systems and processes. If having better results is not the objective, you should reduce the number of people.

"GOVERNMENT OFFICE" TRIANGLE

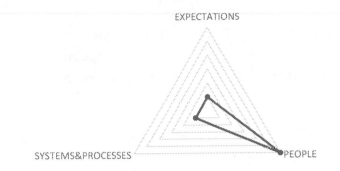

The Switched off High Processor PC situation is like having a powerful PC that is not connected to a power supply. What is the point of having such a powerful PC? If you are in this situation, you are not maximizing your outcomes. If you are lucky enough to have the right system and processes, you can increase expectations and improve your people. If having better results is not the objective, you should reduce your systems.

"SWITCHED OFF HIGH-PROCESSOR PC" TRIANGLE

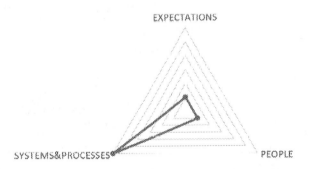

It is important to balance the three elements around you. You must do a conscious and intentional work inside and outside your organization. A majority of managers manage down in their organizations. They manage their people. Few managers are managing up, working with their bosses to correctly set expectations. If you want to be a good manager, you cannot only manage your people. You also need to work with your boss to ensure expectations are balanced, decisions about people are shared, and resources are provided. Many managers are only trying to please their bosses. When you please your boss by accepting unreachable goals, you are part of the imbalance in your business unit. It could be simple and easy to please your boss, but you will have a hard life to manage your people, systems, and processes to deliver.

Draw your triangle and decide how to balance the triangle. You can use the following table to help you.

Area	Current Status	Objective	Actions	Deadline	Next Immediate Action	Who	Monthly Status Review
Expectations	High	Reduce					
People	Low	Improve					
Systems and Processes	Low	Improve					

Think about the following questions:

- How can you improve or lower expectations?
- How can you improve or lower the number or quality of people?
- How can you improve or reduce the performance of your system and processes?

Write down your answers, prepare the table, and start your action plan and monthly reviews. If the whole is not balanced, you will continue to struggle. It is better to work on rebalancing the triangle. When you have a stable equilibrium, you will start to see the results of a more balanced situation. Your performance, your work environment and the work-life balance of your organization will improve.

5.3 ALL-CHAIN ASSESSMENT

Whatever you are managing is part of a bigger organization. You might be managing a department — marketing, sales, operations, finance, or HR. You might be the general manager who is part of a bigger group. You may be managing a cross-functional team that is part of a bigger organization. When you look at the organization, you can always see its parts. The bigger universe contains your organization and external organizations (suppliers, customers, and consumers).

You must be aware of all the parts of the bigger universe and assess them as you have done in the business circle. Doing this exercise will help you clarify weak areas that require intervention. The weak areas might not be under your direct control, but that does not matter. If the vulnerable area is affecting your results, you must find a way to influence positive change. If you cannot directly influence them, you must take some countermeasures to limit the issues. We are always part of something bigger, and we cannot just work to make our own world perfect. If there is something wrong outside your direct area of responsibility, there will be a negative impact on your organization.

The chain requires to assess all the relevant players in your business, in all the parts of the business circle: goals, organization, motivation, processes, systems, discipline, execution, and innovation. After the assessment, you will exactly know which parts require more attention. This tool is a visual way of making sure your efforts are focused on where they matter. Otherwise, you could be spending too much time and effort on fixing or improving the wrong parts of the system.

You can apply the chain I drafted for my work to your reality. My reality was about a commercial B2B subsidiary of a large multinational company. As general manager, I was looking at our organization as the whole subsidiary. I did not split the departments because I was interested in understanding the entire chain — from our subsidiary to the end consumer, passing through customers, owners, managers, and shop staff. This chain has all the steps our product had to go through before getting to consumers. We were selling eyewear as a wholesaler to opticians. Our eyewear products had to be bought by owners since the customers were mostly family businesses. The purchase orders, logistics, and shipments to stores had to be handled by the customers' managers. Once the products reached the store, the shop staff displayed them on the shelves and decided if they were sold or not. Once the product was on the shelves, the end consumer could finally buy it.

Area\Part	Our Internal Organization	Customer's Owner	Customer's Managers	Customer's Shop Staff	End Consumers	Total Score	%
Goals	8	6	4	4	7	29	58%
Organization	6	5	5	6	7	29	58%
Motivation	7	5	4	4	6	26	52%
Processes	5	4	4	4	5	22	44%
Systems	5	2	2	2	2	13	26%
Discipline	6	5	4	4	4	23	46%
Execution	6	5	4	4	5	24	48%
Innovation	5	0	0	0	4	9	18%
Total Score	48/80	32/80	27/80	28/80	40/80	175/400	
%	60%	40%	34%	35%	50%		44%

From the table above, it is possible to draw some conclusions:

- The overall chain delivers a value of 44 percent, which is very far from an acceptable value. This is my subjective evaluation related to my own situation in the country I was operating. Eyewear is not yet an exciting product for many people — even though many need visual correction. We all have at least one smartphone, but fewer people have eyewear. We change smartphones frequently, but eyewear lasts for many years. Manufacturers could do better, retail chains could be more prepared, and shop staff could have better systems and processes. The score (44 percent) represents the overall situation. I am not an expert in other industries, but as a consumer, the overall chain score for smartphones is pretty high. The products are good, and the shops are always in prime areas. The stores look beautiful, and the staff is groomed and prepared.

- The chain is weak on the retail side, and the issue generally starts with poor performance by the retail ownership. There are not enough advanced management practices to manage with a scientific approach. Chains are owned by families but generally fail to grow their management skills. The low performance is usually reflected in the managers and staff. They are not motivated and equipped with old-fashioned tools in most cases.

- The end consumer will probably face an unmotivated and unskilled shop staff with no access to good retail systems. This area requires immediate intervention. Without good staff, the products will not sell. You can have the best product on the shelves, but if the shop assistant is not able to explain why the end consumer should buy it, that product will remain there. Based on this assessment, I chose to have a strong training plan and develop better knowledge for the stores staff about our products and brands. Another strategic decision was investing in incentive programs to motivate staff to sell our products.

- Processes and systems are an issue. Those areas cannot be changed in the short term and require strong sponsorship from owners. I always tried to influence customers to upgrade. We had some success in convincing some retail chains to adopt a new system provided by our company.

- Innovation scored the lowest everywhere, but I did not consider it a key concern for middle managers. Innovation should come from entrepreneurs. A manager should focus on more pragmatic areas. Breakthrough innovations will not come from managers unless shareholders, big corporations, and industry leaders decide to do so. Otherwise, it could come from outsiders who bring other ways of doing business to the industry. At the moment, e-commerce could be a serious alternative to the more common optician store.

Even if I could score 80/80 in my internal organization, the overall chain would still have serious problems. Instead of perfecting my organization, I decided to put more time and effort into improving the rest of the chain, at least for what I could influence.

This tool can help you develop a quantitative assessment of the bigger picture. Having a good understanding of where you operate is an important skill. When you do your chain, always keep the areas to assess in rows instead of columns. Put the parts in column from left to right in order of what is before and after you. I have put my subsidiary (internal organization) in the first column. I could have put our headquarters and the regional office in separate columns, on the left of my subsidiary.

If you are managing a department, you can prepare the chain with the departments that are before and after yours.

If you do not want to have too many columns, consider the parts that are relevant to you. If a production manager were doing an assessment, the shop staff would not be a key part to assess.

Once the matrix is done and the weak areas have been identified, write down a plan for the next immediate actions. This matrix can be a valid tool for your planning phase.

5.4 IT'S TIME FOR ACTION

Think about your business.

- Which areas require improvement? Goals, motivation, organization, processes, systems, discipline, execution, innovation are all good? Prepare your Business Circle.
- Is your business unit coherent among expectations, people, systems, and processes? Any imbalance? Prepare your Business Triangle.
- When you look beyond your business unit, what is the status there? Do you need to work to improve some areas that are before or after your team? Or is it enough to work just on your team? Prepare your All-Chain assessment.

6

NEGOTIATING

Did you know? You negotiate every day, even if you are not in sales. But how do you negotiate professionally? Negotiation is a key skill for every manager. Everybody is negotiating to get something. Many times, different parties will have different interests, wants, needs, and views of a problem or an opportunity. In the end, a party will think A, and another will think B, and another will think C — or in the worst case, Z. When views are similar, it is easy to reach an agreement. In other cases, opposite views will prolong negotiations or eliminate agreements. Negotiation is required to find the agreement. If you are involved with external parties, read books, listen to podcasts, and follow specific courses on how to negotiate. Once you know the basics of negotiation, you reach agreements with others more easily. It is a skill used daily. It is important to have at least the basics. There is nothing difficult about negotiation. It may seem complicated, but it can be learned. With some training, you can avoid basic mistakes.

6.1 KEEP THIS IN MIND WHEN NEGOTIATING

Do not get stuck in your position. Do not fight to win by knocking down the counterpart. It is not a boxing fight. You will never get one hundred percent of what you want if the other party is not happy. Close the negotiation with an agreement. It is not you winning, and the other party losing. In a negotiation, you do not have to prove you are the strongest or the smartest. It is about reaching an agreement. Do not get stuck in your position. You want something, and they want something else. The point is to reach an agreement on what both parties want as "we." You will go into a negotiation with some wants, and the other party will have some other wants. If you are successful, the negotiation will end up with what both parties want. Make sure there is a **mutual interest** to honor the agreement between you and the counterpart. There must be a reward for both parties if the agreement is honored. There must be a punishment if the agreement is not honored. Never put yourself in a situation where there are only rewards and no punishments for your counterpart. You will be risking not getting what you want. If the other party does not have a punishment or loss for not honoring the agreement, they can walk away with zero repercussions. This will put more pressure on you in the future. Many customers say, "My word is gold" or "My words count more than a contract.", but still you better have the agreement formalized. You are doing a good job for your company if you protect your company. It is not a matter of not trusting the other party. Let them understand that you appreciate that you can count on them, but you need a written agreement with conditions that clearly show the agreed-upon terms.

Write down all the details of the agreement in a document. Do not leave your agreement undocumented. Ask them to sign the document and circulate it by email to the relevant people in the negotiation.

At the beginning of my career as a general manager, I was looking only at my perspective. I was looking at what I thought was in the best interests of both parties. That was a mistake. Even if my proposal was close to the optimum solution for both, the other party was challenging and prolonging the negotiation based on their point of view.

You probably want to close the negotiation quickly, but some negotiations take a long time. You must be prepared to be patient. The best use of time is to uncover the needs, wants, and non-negotiable issues of the other party. Before proposing your offer, spend time understanding what the other party wants. You need to be able to write down what they want in order of priority. If you cannot write it down, you do not know it yet.

The easiest way to uncover what they want is to ask. Ask an open question about their areas of interest. What do they value most in doing business with you? What do they expect from you? Once you are clear, you can see the gap versus what you want. For some points, it will be easy to reach an agreement. For others, it will take longer. Once what "they want" and what "you want" are clear, you will define which areas to negotiate.

In every negotiation, there will be a party with more negotiation power. Someone is in a position of strength, and the other one is weaker. In some cases, the difference in power is so high that there is no negotiation at all. The stronger party will impose its will on the weaker one. In most cases, the power is distributed. In an ideal situation, you have more power or are equal in power. The weaker you are, the more you have to accept the other's will.

I wrongly believed that my rational approach to the negotiation could erase the level of power when my company accounted for less than ten percent of the business of a customer. They were a big portion of our business and were so important to our business that the negotiation would always be tough.

The difficult part is determining which areas to negotiate. You could be negotiating in an area that is not interesting at all for the other party! If you look only at your interests, you will go in circles — and nothing will get done because you are negotiating in the wrong area. Discover what the other party wants, start negotiating, and do not try to impose your point of view on the other party or they will walk away.

You can prepare a graph to help you visualize the situation. Below a graph for my case described before.

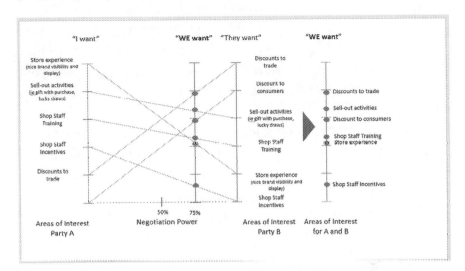

- Rank the areas of interest by priority for both parties.
- Draw a line where the negotiation power is based on your assessment of which party has more power. Halfway between A and B is equal power (fifty/fifty). I assessed party B to have seventy-five percent of the power in the negotiation.
- Connect the priorities between the two parties.
- In the "we want" line, you have the areas of interest to be negotiated.

I was negotiating for days to improve a customer's stores, but it was not important for them. Since they had so much negotiation power, I should have agreed on a decent discount for them since that was their top priority, in return of improving our brands' presence in their stores. It seems easy now, but I wish I had it five years ago. I would have saved a lot of time, and the business would have been probably much bigger. I wasted so much time defending my position. If I had been working on what they wanted, it would have been much more productive.

The graph shows the areas of interest to negotiate upon. It does not say that you should give in and offer the other party everything they want. It shows which areas you need to be ready to negotiate and the order of priority. When you are clear on those areas, you will work better with your team. You will avoid asking them to work on long presentations and offers for something the customer does not value. If you work in the right areas, the customer will be happier, and your team will be more thrilled too. You will reach a faster agreement, and everyone will be satisfied.

If you have a non-negotiable issue, you need to state it at the beginning. Be clear on what you are not going to negotiate. Do not fall into the trap of negotiating non-negotiable issues. You must be clear with yourself and hold yourself accountable. If you open the door to a possible negotiation, it is not a non-negotiable issue.

6.2 TYPES OF BUSINESS RELATIONSHIPS

Many people, like me, are naturally inclined to think everyone is cooperative and honors agreements. If you have this type of inclination, you have to realize that not everyone is like you. You will be disappointed when someone else behaves uncooperatively. It all comes down to trust. Trust is a matter that involves every part of the business: it exists or not between colleagues, with the boss, with other departments, but also between your company, customers, and suppliers.

If you are managing a department or a company, you are not the owner. You cannot trust words, good intentions, or your gut feeling. You need more proof. You need to prove that the agreement foresees rewards for both parties, but also penalties for the party that breaks the agreement.

The best way to honor agreements is to have a mutual interest among the parties. If the interest is mutual, there is a high chance the agreement will be honored from your counterpart. If mutual interest is absent, the chance is near to zero. Trust must be earned. You cannot give it to anyone for free. Trust those who already showed they could be trusted. Always make sure there is a mutual interest to cement the agreement.

If there is no mutual interest, you might wake up one day without an agreement. You could spend months or years over a deal and see it disappear overnight. In the absence of mutual interest, you are the one who will bear the costs and consequences. The other party will walk away with no scars. You could have wasted money, time, and hopes in the negotiations. You could have introduced wrongly more benefits and no punishments for the counterpart. You could have even encouraged the other party to repeat the bad behavior for the next time.

The other characteristic to look at is the level of cooperation from the other party. You will find cooperative counterparts and uncooperative ones. With cooperative counterparts, agreements are easy to reach, business proceeds exactly as per the agreement, and they execute on time and with the quality they committed to. They probably see a future that is similar to your vision. Others may do exactly the opposite. They challenge your proposals, do not respond to offers, and may reject without feedback. When the agreement is reached, they may be late. They even could refer to a different understanding of the agreement, showing that you are the one who misinterpreted. Putting the level of mutual interest and the cooperation level in a matrix is possible to discover four basic types of business relationships:

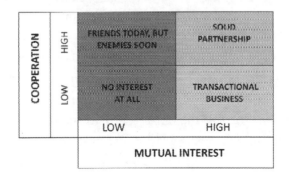

83

6.2.1 Solid Partnerships

This is the ideal state, but it is not the norm. Both parties have a strong mutual interest to honor the agreement and cooperate in the execution. Keep this ideal state in mind and try to move the other three situations toward this one. When you work on those two axes — putting in place real actions to improve mutual interest and cooperation — you will have a smoother future. You must maintain the business partners who are already in this box. You can regularly celebrate the results together with them, find ways to make the work more fun, and spend time together after a meal. You can plan off-site sessions to work on future projects or leisure activities.

6.2.2 Transactional Business

There is mutual interest, but your counterpart does not cooperate. This could happen for several reasons: lack of skills, being too busy with other projects, inability to focus, not feeling entirely comfortable doing business with you, or trying to show their power. You have to invest yours and your organization's time to make sure the execution of the agreement happens along the agreed timeline. You have to supervise. Establish regular checkpoints and reviews (weekly, biweekly, or monthly depending on the situation). Write down everything that is agreed to and document every step detailing who is doing what by when and how. You cannot live in this situation forever because it will drain your energy. You need to find ways to improve cooperation levels. If it is a matter of personal relationships, get to know them better, understand their KPIs, or learn what will help them to be more cooperative. Ask them what could facilitate better cooperation. If you can find the cause, it is easier to find the cure. If it is a matter of lack of skills, you can offer help with tasks or invest in training for their people. If it is a matter of a busy schedule, you can lock in their schedule for the next few months in advance and avoid never-ending meetings. If someone inside their organization does not feel comfortable doing business with you, you can try to understand why and decide if you want to invest the time to improve or accept the situation as it is. If it is a matter of showing their power, there is not much you can do. It is difficult to change ego issues. In this case, probably just let them perceive they are more important than you. Until you do not move to a better situation, always ensure the agreement is executed as planned, every step along the way.

6.2.3 Friends Today, Enemies Tomorrow

If the counterpart is cooperative but lacks mutual interest, they might withdraw sooner or later their commitment. This can happen if you did not introduce for the other party any punishment for not honoring the agreement. Maybe you only included a reward. While things are good, they will cooperate. As soon as something changes, you will be disappointed. They will be your enemy. To avoid this, strengthen mutual interest. If you only have rewards for your counterpart, you need to find a way to introduce penalties.

6.2.4 No Interest at All

A relationship does not exist if there is no mutual interest or cooperation. If you are the only party interested in the relationship, you will invest a lot of time and effort and get nothing in return. Do not invest your energies. Stay away. Spend time and efforts in more productive situations. If your business depends strongly on that specific counterpart, try to work on the mutual interest first. Cooperation will come later. With a customer, for example, you can introduce a strong incentive to achieve a purchase target. The incentive must be so strong that it will also be a loss if the agreement is not reached.

You can look for ways to show how much unique value you can bring to your counterpart. In the absence of a distinctive value, you do not have any leverage. In this case, the temptation is to get business based on purely personal relationships. This strategy can be good for short-term business, but it is not a long-term sustainable strategy.

It is important to assess what kind of relationship you are in. Your level of investment must be in line with the situation. Do not invest the same level of effort, time, and money in every relationship. After the assessment is done, decide which actions must be taken to bring the relationship to a new level. Do not let the relationship drive you. You must drive the relationship.

If you are the party who is not cooperative, ask yourself why and decide if the relationship is worth keeping. Be honest, transparent, and clear with the other party. If you are not interested, an act of honesty will avoid wasting yours and your counterpart's time. You will also save the time and energy of your team that will not be working with counterparts who are not important to your business. Politely share to your counterpart that you have no interest in the relationship.

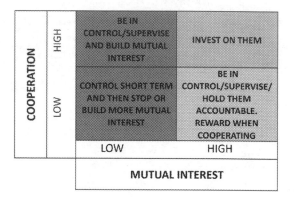

6.3 IT'S TIME FOR ACTION

Think about your business.

- Do you have mutual interest with your business partners?
- Are there rewards for your business partners to keep their commitments?
- Are there punishments for your business partners if they fail in their commitments?
- Which types of business relationship do you have with your key partners? Anything to improve?

7

YOUR MANAGEMENT STYLE

You are tall, average, or short. This will not change. You do not have the leverage to influence your height. But when it comes to your management style, you can often change, depending on the situation. You do not have only one management style. You are not defined by one style.

7.1 WHICH MANAGEMENT STYLE IS RIGHT?

I had to ask myself this question when I was assigned to manage a new subsidiary. My first field assignment was with a startup. I had to build everything from scratch, including the team. My second assignment was taking over an existing team. I was working virtually with the new team in the new country, and it was important to define how I would manage both countries. I could not dedicate myself one hundred percent to a single country. I had to decide on the best management style to apply. I came up with a simple answer that helped me find my way. I assessed the maturity stage of the two countries based on why, how, who, when, and what:

- Does the organization know why it exists? Are the purpose, vision, and goals clear?
- Do the people know how to work? Are working processes and tools in place?
- Are the team members the right ones? Do they have the right skills and mindsets to deliver?
- Are the team members disciplined enough to deliver on-time results?
- Are the team members able to deliver the expected results?

I was able to define which management style I should adopt. In the country where I started, the team was quite good after four years. They were clear on their purpose, vision, and goals. They had good processes in place, and we changed already the nonperformers. The team was equipped with good people and was constantly delivering with high discipline and respecting timelines. The team was able to deliver results, and they frequently overachieved.

The new country was in a different phase. They were clear on the why, but they lacked good working processes. The team was keeping nonperformers, which resulted in not delivering results and no discipline.

According to the five questions, I decided to delegate a lot in the first country. I was mostly encouraging, coaching, and giving direction. In the new country, I had to start by building working processes. I started with how and moved to other aspects. I worked on the new processes required, defining every step, redefining who was doing what and when, finding new ways of doing things.

The other area was in the who. We had to let go of a team member due to poor performance and hire a new person who demonstrated much better performance. It was about also working on developing the skills and mindsets of the rest of the team.

Working on the when was also important. It was important to follow through and make sure deadlines were respected. I helped the team manage its time, reminded them about upcoming deadlines, and made sure everything explained so far in this book was in place. After a few months, the team started to deliver. The signs of improvements were visible and had continued to improve.

The way I framed the questions above helped me take the right steps to improve the situation. It can help you assess your situation too. Ask yourself those questions in that order, and when your answer is that you are not satisfied, then you found the starting point.

The most difficult part is when the team does not know why they exist. This is normal in a startup, but it can happen with established teams that have not been directed well. If the team is in this situation, you have to start from scratch. Your key tasks will be sharing the vision, goals, priorities, key success factors, and strategies. You cannot expect good performance from people who do not understand why they are working. Would you work well on a task or project that you did not understand?

You have to build systems, processes, and a team. You have to demonstrate the proper behaviors for delivering on-time results. It is a difficult stage, but you need to work on all the aspects to deliver good results. You need to have full involvement in everything until you move to the next stages. Be emotionally prepared for your own stretched effort. I have been in that situation, and I moved to all the next steps. I sometimes felt like I was not good enough, and I sometimes felt overwhelmed. After a couple of years, I started to see improvements. Today, when I look back, I see that it was the best moment in my professional life. What you learn in that phase is gold. You are exposed to every aspect of the business. Only managers who experience this phase and succeed have a chance to understand all the aspects of a business. If you are in that situation, live it with joy. You will learn and become stronger — maybe even the strongest.

If your team is not working efficiently and effectively due to a lack of processes and tools, you need to help to build them. When processes and tools are not optimized, your team is wasting time and is not productive. To get more done, you need better processes and tools.

You need to go into the details, and you need to see with your eyes and test yourself. This does not mean you need to work on the process and tools with your own hands. You can delegate to others to come up with new ways, but you still need to supervise and frequently check that improvements are happening. You want to speed up this phase. Once your people are working efficiently, they will start to be more productive. If the team is in this situation, it means there are issues with the team members as well. Otherwise, if the team members were the right ones and working well, they would have fixed the processes already. Anyhow, you have to deliver business. You have to do a lot yourself in this phase. You have to build your team and develop skills and mindsets. When processes are not in place your business is not guaranteed. Be careful. You need to step in in many specific aspects. You will do a lot of micromanaging, but if it is temporary, it is okay. You are always responsible for results. When you fix processes, you will start to achieve results.

If the issue is about team composition, you have to find replacements for those who are not the right fit. You have to improve the skills and mindsets of those who have the potential to be good performers. In a weekly meeting, go through all the open projects and priorities to see if the team is progressing in the right direction and at the right speed. It is important to coach people about how you want the job done. This is a key part of developing skills and mindset since you have all team members in the same room at the same time. Of course, one-on-one meetings will be required too.

You will dedicate more frequent one-on-one meetings to team members who are behind. You will ensure the team member is delivering what is expected, and it is a great chance to correct any gaps, develop skills, and work on their mindset. Team meetings and one-on-one meetings will be the backbone of this phase. As you build the team, you will build good relationships and learn aspects of team members' personal lives. Get to know them — and let them get to know you. Try to schedule off-site lunches and dinners. Spending time with people outside of the office is an invaluable tool for building a good team dynamic.

If your team is already clear on the why, the how, and the who, but struggles in delivering on time, you have to help them with time management. It is probably an issue of behavior or discipline. You can make sure timelines are set, and deadlines are respected. You can help the team with early reminders about upcoming deadlines.

If the team is proposing a deadline that is too far off, you have to see which projects can be delivered faster. They will appreciate that you are willing to listen and are interested in finding ways to help them respect deadlines. To reinforce that you expect results always to be delivered on time, you can use many occasions to reinforce this message. For example, meetings have to start and finish at the scheduled time. Meetings have to be scheduled for everyone in the calendar, and if they are canceled, the new schedule must be reflected in the calendar. I have seen many team members writing emails to set meetings but not scheduling in Outlook. I consider that a sign of a lack of discipline. If it is not in Outlook, how can people remember the meeting? The sender or receiver will probably forget about the meeting. If the meeting is canceled, the sender might not cancel the meeting in Outlook. If the meeting is not canceled in Outlook, someone will think the meeting is still on.

I always ask my team to use Outlook and update the calendar. Just by doing this, the team will understand the importance of time. Your team should use a shared weekly file where all actions are listed with owners and deadlines. If something is on the calendar, people will remember it. With smartphones and smartwatches, if the team is disciplined, there are no excuses for forgetting. Use technology to help the team.

There is a cultural aspect of time to consider. Different cultures value time in different ways. If you are managing in a culture where deadlines are not so important, and delays are acceptable, you need to understand how to communicate the importance of delivering on time. Even if you manage a culture where delays are acceptable, I do not suggest adapting. To succeed as a manager, you need to shorten the time between ideas and actions. If you accept late actions, you are not performing at your best. If you are in those cultures, agree with the team on a realistic timeline, but it must be respected.

The ideal situation is when your team is already clear on the how, why, who, and when. If those elements are already in place, the *what* will happen. However, even if you are lucky to be in this situation, do not think the team will do everything without you. You have to ensure that the organization is working properly, without conflicts, and with clarity of action. You have to encourage your team members and spread positive energy. In the case of setbacks, you have to motivate your team to move forward. You will always have to be there for advice.

If you are in that phase, it means everything else is already in place. You have done an excellent job and is now a matter of maintenance. Do not think that the game is over. However, your professional life is more relaxed and comfortable than the previous stages since you should not have a lot of issues on your to-do list. You probably are ready for your next step. But until the next step arrives, you are still the manager and responsible for your team.

This table summarizes the management style to adopt, depending on the situation of your team:

Stage	Focus on	The Team Is Here If	The Manager Focuses On	Management Style
1	why	purpose, vision, and goals are not clear	setting up all, clarifying purpose, vision, goals, and priorities	full control
2	how	working processes and tools are not good	building systems and processes	build team, control business, control behaviors, build processes and tools
3	who	team members are not performing or are not the right people	picking the right people and developing skills and mindsets of team members	build team, control business and control behaviors
4	when	the team does not deliver on time	providing deadlines and following up on deadlines	monitor business and control behaviors
5	what	all the previous factors are okay	agreeing on objectives, monitoring achievements, offering encouragement, and coaching.	delegate business and monitor results

Once you understand which situation you are in, it is a matter of preparing your action plan, next immediate action, and action review. Do not stop analyzing where you are. Write down what you have to do — and start doing it!

7.2 AVOID COMPLEXITY

Simplicity is important. My company had "simple" in its core values. It was quite natural for me to grow up professionally with this in mind. Just because a company has simplicity as a core value does not mean that complexity does not happen. I have always been a simple guy, and I have always tried to keep things simple.

Many years ago, I had a chance to have a one-on-one meeting with the CEO of my company. The CEO asked me: "What do you think I am doing well?." It was a simple question to answer. I had seen him in many meetings in the previous six years, and he was always going for the essence of a problem or the essence of an opportunity He brought simplicity to everything he was doing and discussing. I told him that simplicity was what he was doing well. He was always bringing the simplest ideas to the table. I could not believe it. I did not think a CEO could be paid to bring simplicity as a key value. When I became a general manager, I learned that simplicity is a key factor for success. There are two ways of reaching simplicity. One is to have your brain naturally wired for it. Another way is to intentionally avoid complexity. If you are in the first situation, you are lucky. Do not feel bad when other people are saying many sophisticated things, showing big projects, busy timelines, busy slides, or talking about complex, sophisticated topics. You are the one who will help the organization keep simplicity alive.

If simplicity is not natural to you, are you thinking in complex ways? Are your ideas simple to execute? Which complexities will the organization face when executing them? Are there simpler ways of executing?

Not everything is simple. Your team will face both complex and simple issues. The key part is in the execution. You need a conscious and intentional effort to make things simple. Execute with simplicity — even if the issue is complex — and the results will be good.

Nature of the Issue	Execution	You Are
Simple	Simple	Great
Complex	Simple	Champion
Simple	Complex	Disaster
Complex	Complex	Disaster

It should be a simple matrix to understand. If the issue is simple, and your execution is simple, you are doing great. If the issue is complex, but you can simplify, go at the essence, and execute with simplicity, you are a champion.

If the situation is simple or complex, but you complicate the execution, you are not doing well. Many managers fail to recognize simple situations that require simple solutions. I have seen projects becoming overcomplicated with too many parts, too many parties, and too many details.

A common mistake for managers is to think about a project on PowerPoint slides, sitting behind a desk in a comfortable chair, in an office with good air-conditioning. Filling PowerPoint slides can be one of the best ways to overcomplicate things. Slides will probably not look good and not be long enough if the execution is too simple. This is why many managers present too many complicated slides, to learn afterward when field teams will execute, all the limits of the real world.

Sadly, many managers are not living the reality of their field teams. Spending too much time in the office and too much time with other managers do not help them have a clear understanding of what is pragmatic and doable and what is not. Your role as a manager is to shorten the time between ideas and action. Simplicity is the enabler of action. Complexity is an obstacle. Fight with all your energies when you see complexity on your team, with your subordinates, with your peer managers, or with your management. Any source of complexity is not good for you — even if it is coming from the top.

You could scan your activities and your team member's activities by following the below framework. List the activities, assign levels of importance to achieve your outcomes, and define the execution as simple or complex. Some activities are not important, but complicated to execute. What is the point of doing those activities in that way? Is there a simpler way of doing it? Could be possible to cut them out completely?

Nature of the Issue	Importance	Execution	Action Required
Activity A	High	Complex	Simplify
Activity B	Average	Simple	Keep it simple
Activity C	Low	Complex	Cut or simplify?

7.3 AVOID MISCOMMUNICATION

Clear communication is another key part of being a good manager. You need to ensure the receiver of your message clearly understands what you want. If messages are not understood, learn more about communication:

- Be clear with yourself first. What do you want? Are you clear about what you want to achieve?
- Check if the receiver is the right one. Are you speaking to the right person? Are you talking to the right team?
- Are you communicating at the right time? If you are communicating too late, everybody will rush to act on what you want, but it will be a chaotic execution at best. If you are communicating too early, people will soon forget what you said.
- Which medium did you choose? Face-to-face meetings, phone, emails, messages? Is it the right medium? Is that medium the one preferred by the receiver? Do not look at

what you prefer; instead, select the preferred channel of the receiver.

Communication requires a lot of attention and it is a very well-known and well discussed topic in management. Misunderstandings and banalities are instead underestimated in management literature.

7.4 AVOID MISUNDERSTANDINGS

Another common issue that can happen is about misunderstandings. You want to communicate a message, but the other person — or the entire team — cannot understand what your message is. Poor communication can cause misunderstandings. Communication is simply about one party sending a message and another party receiving the message. However, a misunderstanding can happen if the message is not sent well or is not received well. For example, you might use some words that are incorrect when you speak a non-native language. You might talk to someone with a different background, like when salespeople talk to finance people. The issue can worsen if the receiver does not ask to clarify any confusion.

A misunderstanding can happen when you assume the other party understood you. At the beginning of my career, I often experienced misunderstandings. I thought *I already explained this to you. How come you did not understand? And if you didn't understand, why didn't you ask me to clarify?*

The most common reaction is claiming no responsibility and blaming the other party. That is not the proper reaction for a manager. You need to take responsibility for clear communication. You need to do more than just communicate — you need to make sure others understand your message. Do not assume you are always clear and that others always understand.

- Accept the fact that misunderstandings can happen and will happen.

- Take one hundred percent responsibility for misunderstandings. There was something wrong in the communication — sending the message or understanding the message — and you are responsible.

You must confirm that the receiver understood your message. Even if your message is correct and explained thoroughly, if the receiver did not understand, nothing will happen. Do not just take care of sending a clear, well-structured message. Be sure to take care of a qualitative understanding of your message.

- Evaluate the clarity of your oral message. Be clear. Do not leave any areas for doubt.
- Ask to the receiver if your message was clear and if there is anything that needs to be clarified. If not, ask them to summarize your message.
- Write down your message and ask the receiver to write down a summary for you.
- Utilize the minutes of the meeting. Be specific and detailed. List all important topics.
- Always ask your receiver to come to you for clarification. Do not let the fear of feeling stupid to prevent them from coming to you.
- When a misunderstanding happens, take the opportunity to discuss what you should do in the future to avoid similar situations.

7.5 AVOID BANALITIES

I often see people who are not prepared to discuss topics that were actually already discussed. My boss visited my business unit from time to time, and I discovered the importance of avoiding banalities. The situation was always the same — a meeting with the leadership team of our business unit — and it always came down to a simple question from him that the team was not able to answer. Their bodies were present, but their brains were somewhere else. Talented, skilled people would give the wrong answer to a common question. I wondered how it was possible that smart people would find it difficult to answer a banal question that had been answered a long time ago.

I thought, *Did you forget that this is exactly what you are doing right now? Why don't you answer? I know you know it!*

I felt sorry for the person who was uncomfortable — and I felt bad for myself. I thought I was doing a great job of leading the team in the best way possible. Instead, those moments reminded me that I was not doing the best that I could.

The main problem was how I was looking at the issue. I was not spending enough time discussing the topics with my team members. It was banal for me, but it was not banal for them. In school, was there someone in the class who could not learn something easy for you? Was a certain topic difficult for you — but others learned it pretty easily?

In the workplace, it is exactly the same. You and your team will face situations were banalities arise. You should be in a good position if you are doing everything described so far in this book: vision, goals, action plans, debriefings, and managing people. Anyhow, a mistake on a banality can strike at any point in time, but that is not the end of the world. When it happens, do not let this event hamper the team's confidence — and maybe your confidence as well.

A simple matrix, call it the Banality Checklist, will help you avoid banalities. Start ranking the banalities by importance. Important topics that your team must always be clear on should be on top. You can do this exercise every day by noticing which topics your team does not fully master. Meetings with management or customers will also be sources for writing down your list of banalities. Write them down, tackle them immediately, and do not think they will disappear.

Banality Checklist	Importance	Current Risk	Corrective Actions	Deadline	Next Immediate Action	Who	Monthly Status Review
Banality A	Top	Low					
Banality B	High	High					
Banality C	Average	High					
Banality D	Low	High					

You need to make a conscious and intentional effort to address the issues with your team. There is probably something bigger behind the banality. If a team member was not ready to answer, there is perhaps more the team member did not understand. People do not just switch off their brains for a while. If they do not know how to answer, they do not know the answer. You can discuss these topics in a debriefing session after the meeting or in one-on-one sessions with your team members. Do not let the banality be there the next time.

7.6 IT'S TIME FOR ACTION

Think about your business.

- Is your management style appropriate considering the situation your business unit is?
- Any complexities?
- Any miscommunications?
- Any misunderstandings?
- Any banalities?

PART II

EMOTIONAL

8

YOU

A manager plays a multitude of roles. You become a good one when you can naturally play many. You need to understand yourself and understand how to manage yourself. You need to know how you see yourself in your organization. What role are you playing? Which roles you are not playing? Which role do you want to play? Depending on how you see yourself, you will have thoughts and actions as a consequence. Everything starts with you and within you. This is the reason why I ask you to think deeply about how you think about yourself. You will soon understand how important you are in your organization.

Part II is about who you are. It is subjective, but I will explain how I see the role of the manager.

8.1 THE DRIVER

After a couple of years as general manager, I figured out the manager is like a driver. Everything starts with a simple question: "When you drive your family or friends, what do they expect from you?"

When you drive, you have a great responsibility for the safety of your passengers and so much more. Your passengers expect the following:

1. you know how to drive
2. arrive safely
3. arrive at the right place
4. arrive at the right time
5. accelerate or brake when needed
6. drive on the right roads
7. drive safely
8. drive comfortably
9. stop to rest along the way
10. talk along the way
11. know what to do in case of an emergency

Expectations as Driver	Expectations as Manager
know how to drive	know how to lead and manage
arrive safely	achieve results smoothly
arrive at the right place	achieve results
arrive at the right time	achieve results on time
accelerate or brake when needed	manage the speed and energy of the team
drive on the right roads	know the right direction
drive safely	manage and lead securely
drive comfortably	manage and lead calmly
stop to rest along the way	manage people's energies
talk along the way	build rapport with your team members
know what to do in case of an emergency	know how to manage a crisis

As a manager, people expect from you:

- Results: you are responsible — not others.
- Skills: you have all the skills to do your job.
- Disciplined execution: you need to achieve on-time and with accuracy
- Direction: you need to decide what to do and when
- Control: you need to be calm and secure.
- Positive: you need to build an environment for employees and stakeholders where they can work at ease.
- Energetic: you need to build rapport with people, manage their energies, and know when to push and when to reduce pressure.
- Crisis management: in a crisis, you need to take the lead.

What happens if passengers pressure the driver with continuous instructions? Should the driver follow the passenger's instructions? The driver is responsible for safely bringing all passengers to the right destination. In the end, whatever the driver decides to do is his responsibility. He must drive in the way he feels is right. He could follow the advice of other passengers, but it is always his responsibility. If he does not want to follow that advice, it is okay. Similarly, the manager is in charge and is responsible for reaching the goal. Others might give advice, but the decision is always up to the manager. Nobody else is responsible.

New managers will hear advice and instructions from management, peers, and subordinates. Being a manager exposes you to many stakeholders, and everyone has a say. You have to be crystal clear that nobody else is in charge but you. Do not blindly follow what others are telling you to do, including your boss. You need to assess if it is the right thing to do and if it will help you and your team achieve your goals.

You will never be excused for making a wrong decision because you followed someone else's advice or instruction. In case of failure, you cannot say, "My boss told me to do that" or "I have done what Mr. or Ms. X told me to do."

You are in charge — you and only you. Receiving advice is helpful, and you can ask for suggestions. You have people who can help you make better decisions. However, in the end, the final decision is your responsibility. Do not let others decide for you.

8.2 THE MAGNET

A magnet can attract iron. I kept a magnet on my desk, and I was curious about what caused the magnet to attract the iron. Why didn't it attract other materials? On the internet, I discovered some lessons that also apply to managers. In short, a magnet attracts iron due to the different direction of atoms. In a piece of magnet, all the electrons are oriented in the same direction. In a piece of iron, instead, electrons are oriented randomly.

A manager cannot be like iron. A manager cannot be randomly oriented. A manager cannot change direction all the time. A manager needs to act like a magnet — aligned in one direction and able to line up in the same direction your team members. If you do not act as a magnet, each of your team members will choose its direction, generating chaos.

As the electrons in iron, the normal state of an organization is chaos and disorder. A state of order can only be achieved with the intervention of an external force. You represent that force. The magnet is in a state of order, as its electrons are aligned in the same direction. Acting like a magnet by adding order to your business gives your organization a chance for success. If you leave things as they naturally are, you are setting up your organization to fail. You must add discipline to your organization by using rational tools that help your organization succeed.

This leads to other considerations:

- To expect discipline from others, you must be disciplined. Everything starts with you. Your organization will mirror you.
- If you are disciplined, you can discipline your business.
- Materials that have been exposed to magnets can become magnetic! When you are disciplined, your team members will spread discipline to the rest of your organization.

However, not all materials, for example copper, wood and plastic, are attracted to a magnet. In your organization, some elements are not going to line up with your given direction. For example, toxic team members that do not have ideas or action power. Or those that have extrinsic motivation, no skills, potential, and discipline. You cannot direct those people — just as the magnet cannot direct a piece of wood. The faster you understand your team members' ability to line up, the faster you understand if you can produce effects. You might have people on your team who are not aligned with your direction, and that is normal, but you need to agree with them on a direction they can follow without randomly going in their own direction.

Having your business in order allows you to achieve objectives in a consistent, solid, and constructive way. Success becomes a consequence of what you have done. In a state of disorder, success is still possible, but it requires luck. There are many more chances to fail.

How do you help the team find order? Share your purpose, vision, and reason for existence. Set goals and priorities, define your action plan and the next immediate action, and constantly review your actions. Display disciplined execution, effective time management, and efficient processes and systems. If a team member does not want to work in that direction, there are four alternatives:

- The company changes direction. That can only happen if the team member can see better than the company.
- The team member changes direction.
- The team member leaves.
- The manager changes direction or leaves.

8.3 YOU ARE BUILDING THE TRACK

In 2009, Usain Bolt set the world record for the hundred-meter dash in 9.58 seconds. Do you think he would be as fast in the mud? He would be slow or completely stuck. Consider your people as the runner and the conditions you put in place for your people as the track. Your job is to build the right conditions for others to perform. You might have a talented team and people who are motivated, skilled, and disciplined. If the environment does not put them in condition, will they reach their full potential? You are responsible for building those conditions. The conditions must offer the team purpose, vision, goals, priorities, an action plan, and the next immediate action. Find people who want to achieve the same things you want. Otherwise, you stuck in the mud.

Your people use hardware, software, and processes to communicate and make internal and external decisions. When systems and processes are not performing, your people are not performing as well as they could. When you ask your people to perform better and faster, you must put them in a position to work better and faster. Ask yourself what you can do to structurally improve systems and processes. When you work to improve systems and processes, you are investing in your people.

However, you have limited power to build the perfect track. You cannot work alone. You need to connect with the people in your organization who can help you build the perfect conditions. Try to build the best conditions, avoid the mud, and let your people run on a smoother surface.

If Usain Bolt is running in the mud and you are running on a track, you will probably be faster. An average team running in a perfect track will deliver better and faster results than great talents running in the wrong one. Your teams will deliver with or without stars, champions, and geniuses. A majority of people in the world has a normal IQ. However, you can help normal people perform like stars if you build the right conditions for them to perform. There is a lot you can do to help others perform better.

8.4 YOU ARE THE CONDUCTOR

An orchestra conductor directs the musicians but is not playing any instrument. You cannot play the role of anyone else in the organization. You need to refrain from trying to do so. When I started as a manager, I was taking charge of many tasks that should have been done by others. I wanted to make things better and faster, but I was overwhelmed with too many tasks. I was working too many hours, and after a while, I was not contributing much. I was not fresh enough to do the important tasks that could only be done by me. My personal life was disappearing. I used my free time merely to sleep and recover energy. My team members were not productive. They were waiting to do something only after my inputs. They were bored, and they did not feel engaged or valued. They were going to the office with their bodies — but not their brains and souls. They were just there to spend the required eight hours. It was a lose-lose situation.

Luckily, I realized I could not continue that way. I was not performing as a manager. The last thing I wanted was to fail. I started changing myself, and that led me to act more like a conductor. It was not an overnight change. It took time. You cannot do the job of others, even if you could do it better and faster.

It is relatively easy to determine if you are doing the job of others. By looking at your to-do list, you can easily understand if an item is there because you are the only person to do it or because you decided to handle it because you did not trust the person who should be assigned. Refrain from doing the jobs of others. When you feel the instinct to do it, you need to be disciplined to define your action plan to delegate effectively.

How do you get others to do their job? Do you trust others? Tackle the root cause of the issue if you do not. You are not doing your job when you are doing the tasks of others. Also remember that people are not happy to be there for nothing. People want to contribute. People want to do what they are paid for.

You need to be able to delegate. If it does not come naturally to you, read some books about it. You need to be disciplined — and do not procrastinate. Do it now. Start to delegate the tasks to the right people. Go to the rational part of this book and follow all the steps. People want to achieve what you want them to achieve. Make sure it is clear who is doing what and by when. Close the loop delegation-accountability by building the right processes. You will keep people accountable for their duties.

8.5 YOU CAN SEE THE FUTURE

What if I could see the future? For sure, I would be happy to see the final results of a project or a year of business, but it would not be enough. I would feel pleased if it ends with success, but I would be sad with failure. I would like to see the final result, but also all the key moments that happened during the journey. What led to the results? What has been done to get there? What could we have done differently? I would like to know what I did right and what I did wrong. What went wrong? When did it go wrong? I would like to see all the key events.

We cannot see the future, but we can imagine the future. We can envision the results we want and define the key events that lead to success. You can write about your future. I encourage you to do a visualization exercise.

- Go to a quiet room, alone, where you cannot be disturbed.
- Bring a piece of paper and a pen. If you like to write and take notes, choose a good notebook or paper and a nice pen.
- Try to relax. You need to be calm and have no urgent tasks to do. You need to have all the necessary time. Make sure no one can disturb you. Earplugs can block outside noise. Try to find a silent place.
- Take deep breaths until you feel relaxed.
- Imagine a day when a project is concluded. You will know if you have been successful or not. As a general manager, the best date to imagine is January 1 of next year because I will know our sales and profits of the previous year. Imagine a day that is important to you.
- Write down the date you are imagining.
- Write down the key performance indicators that define your success. What defines success for you? Make sure you list what is meaningful for you. This is not about how your

company measures success. This is how you measure success. Ideally, the two are the same.

- Look at the key performance indicators you wrote down and notice how you feel. Which feelings do you have? Are you happy? Joyful? Do you feel satisfied? Do you feel proud of yourself? Do you feel proud of your team? Feel your emotions. Spend as much time as you want to feel your emotions.
- Explore all the moments backward from the day you are envisioning. Think about the key moments for you and your team and write them down. For me, the key moments were the sales events and agreements with customers.
- Imagine those key moments and observe how you feel. After you identify a key moment, move to the next one. Repeat. Feel it again — and move to the following one. Every time you identify a key moment, write it down and label as a reminder of what you imagined. For me, it was our August sales event in Bangkok.
- Go backward until your current month.
- Prepare a table with all the key moments in row. Prepare a column for what is happening in those moments, who is part of the success, and how you and your team worked. Fill in all the boxes.

After this exercise, you should have your road map to success. You have all the key moments, you know what you have to do, and you identified how you would measure success at the end of the project. You wrote down your future. Your table should look like this:

Final Date of Success: January 1 of next year

Final Key Performance Indicators:		**Budget**	**My Future**		
	Sales	X Million	X+ Million		
	Profit	Y Million	Y+ Million		
	Collection	Z days	Z days		

Key Events:		**Moment Name**	**What**	**Who**	**How**
▪	December	Last shipment	Ship by December 10	Sales team	Planned by November
▪	September	Last sales event Q4			
▪	August	Midyear sales event			

Ask yourself if you are happy if the future happens as you have written it. If yes, put it in the goal-clarification map. It is time to share your vision for the future with your team. You need to make that future your reality. What will be your next immediate action? The future is not written by somebody else or by destiny — you make your future every day with every decision or action you do or do not do. The future is in your hands.

8.6 ALWAYS STRIKE: WHY, WHAT, WHEN, WHO, WHERE AND HOW

You can achieve better and faster if you are clear on the why, who, when, where, what, and how. An image that reminds me to be clear on those basic elements is bowling. If you put down all the pins, you strike. Strike every time you need to take action. Strike every day, making sure that for every project, you have defined all the elements.

8.7 SQUEEZED LIKE AN ORANGE EVERY DAY

Pressure will be a natural part of your job. You are hired to deliver results and to do that you have a team. Your organization expects profits, and you are helping your company achieve that. Your company is not a nonprofit organization. Even if you work for a nonprofit, there are other objectives to achieve. Every organization exists to achieve defined objectives.

I am always amazed when I see managers complaining about delivering more results with fewer resources. Profit and loss statements are clear: the objective of any company is to increase revenues and decrease costs. Every department and every manager are required to produce more with less.

Many managers complain unnecessarily about company challenging requests. You need to be comfortable in your situation, and if you are the manager, it means the company believes you can do well. It is a matter of mindset. You can see the company's expectations as a problem or as an opportunity. If your perspective is negative, you will not be successful. You will continue to struggle. Your company will continue to ask for more and give you less. That is not going to change.

You should be worried if the company does not ask you to deliver more. That would be a clear sign that the company is not growing and is not going to be successful. Would you like to work for a company that produces losses instead of profits? What kind of future will you have with that kind of company? Do you expect salary increases every year? Do you expect bonuses? Do you expect the company to invest in training? Do you think you will have a bright career path? These things are available at growing companies. Growing companies will always ask you to deliver more with less. That is the essence of profit. A manager will be squeezed like an orange every day. You will be squeezed to deliver good juice. The faster you accept that you are there to deliver results, the better you will understand your role in the organization. Do not think the company loves you so much and wants to give you a good salary and good benefits because you are nice. Do not think the company should do that because you put in so much effort or have good intentions. As a manager, you must deliver. That's it. Start to feel comfortable under pressure. A manager must feel comfortable in an uncomfortable situation.

As the orange is squeezed in every part, you too will be squeezed from all angles. You will feel requests coming from many parties. Many managers struggle with so many requests. They complain about having so many demands. Many managers think they are the only ones who are allowed to make requests. Many managers think their team members are there to follow orders — but the manager should not be bothered with their requests.

A natural reaction to pressure is pushing back at everyone. Pushing back at your boss can be difficult, but pushing back at requests coming from your subordinates, peers, or team members is relatively easy. You have authority with your team members. You can do it with your peers because you are not directly related to them. Saying no could become your normal way of responding to requests.

You could also wrongly start to overreact by demanding things from others as they continue demanding from you. If you are in this stage, it is not ideal, because others are stressed from your reactions as they do not get what they need. You push back at requests, but sooner or later, your attitude will not be tolerated in the workplace. If you are in this stage and are constantly reacting negatively: stop, relax, and take control of the situation. Managers who do not accept requests from their subordinates and peers will always struggle — and they will not go far in their careers. Do not be one of them.

Few people, when becoming the boss for the first time, don't feel squeezed. They have a natural talent to handle the pressure. However, for the majority of people, it is normal to struggle. The point is that it is not healthy to feel squeezed every day. You have to change how you live with continuous requests. With experience and time, you will feel more comfortable.

The ideal scenario is when you actively work maturely with others and you also comfortably deliver. You can get all the required inputs and necessary information, and you also manage expectations about the right time to deliver. In this stage, you can set realistic expectations and find all the information you need. You are absorbing requests from others, but you are actively working with others to achieve your objectives. In this stage, you move across the organization with ease, and others feel at ease with you.

Sometimes you push back on requests, postpone deadlines, or lower expectations, but most of the times you can comfortably say yes. In this way, the whole — you and others — stays in balance. Others are satisfied, and you are in control. You get what you want, and others get what they want. It is a matter of balancing the whole.

8.8 FROM TASKS TO PEOPLE

There is a difference between leadership and management. Leadership is about doing the right thing, and management is about doing things right. Good leadership is shown in directing the organization toward the right destination. Management is doing the right things to achieve the destination set by the leader.
Several images can show the difference. A leader decides where to put the ladder, and the manager decides how to climb the ladder.

The ladder could be positioned in the wrong direction and lead to nothing. However, you could still have a good manager who will make things happen quickly. An entrepreneur could open a business with no potential, invest their own money, hire a CEO and managers, and ask them to run the business. The CEO and managers will define all the steps to make things happen, but in the end, the business will still have no potential.

This definition does not mean that managers are blind and stupid and will always run in the wrong direction. However, a manager cannot decide to change the vision, mission, bigger purpose, and final destination set by the company. If the CEO does not agree with the founder or shareholders, the CEO will leave. If the CEO was right, that is a different story.

The manager is not the employee and not the leader. The manager is in the middle between them. You must act as expected from a managerial level and keep your skills in tune with your role.

Skills can be split into soft and hard. People management is a key soft skill. Technical knowledge is a key hard skill. This is a simple and common management concept, but not many managers grasp the fundamental distinction between soft and hard skills. Many managers were good employees with good technical skills, but they did not evolve into their new management role. They tend to stick with their technical skills. There is a big issue in business schools and companies. I attended university and earned a master degree from two leading Italian universities, and I was in an exchange program in Canada in an important university. I was working for a multinational company, and I thought I had great business preparation. In reality, when I look back, at school I only learned technical skills. All my people skills were developed on my own through daily experience. When I look at managers, subordinates, and bosses, I can observe that there is no formal, scientific-based education to develop people skills. Being aware of this weakness is half of the solution.

When you were an employee if you had great technical skills you were performing at your best. You were required to have simple people skills. When you were an employee, not a manager yet, you could have had just basic or average teamwork skills. Maybe you were not a good team player either, but your boss did not ask you to improve. You were only required to complete tasks.

As an employee, my bosses never told me how to be a good team member. I was polite, and as I did not bring problems, all was fine. Most employees are not taught how to be good team members. They have to learn about people management when they become managers.

It would be good for companies and business schools to start teaching people how to be good managers and employees.

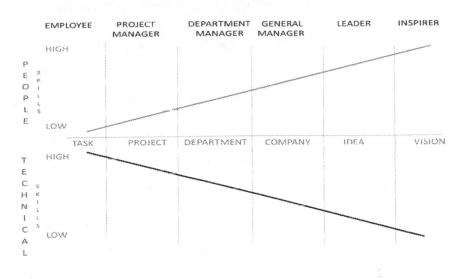

Employee Level

- Employees do tasks. They must have high technical skills, but it is ok if they have low people skills.

Manager Level

- As a project manager, you need a lot of technical skills. You need some people skills to coordinate team members, peers, and superiors. You will not need the same level of technical skills as your team members. If you do not specialize in certain tasks, your team members will.
- As a department manager, you will need technical skills and people skills.
- A general manager can work effectively with no technical knowledge of how employees complete tasks. However, the General Manager must have good people skills to manage a company
- The CEO requires even more people skills.

Leader Level

- A leader can have zero technical skills but have excellent people skills. A leader must inspire people to go in a certain direction. People are not convinced and inspired by technical skills only.

Inspirer Level

- At this level, people skills and powerful ideas are required. This person can inspire people with their ideas. Communication skills are required to manage people effectively.

Managers need people skills. When you are a manager, it is good to have technical skills, but as you advance in your career, you need to become better at working with others. The essence of management is knowing how to work effectively with others.

We can try to categorize people, understand people, and adapt our styles. To advance in your career path, you must have good people skills. The sooner you learn, the better. People management is something you can learn through education or experience. Try to notice what works best in your daily interactions with people. Adapt to others. Find a way to work with others. Make a conscious and intentional effort. Do not think that people skills are a talent that cannot be learned.

Always check where you are. Ask yourself if you are balancing correctly people and technical skills. Take a monthly or quarterly self-reflection and take action if a change is needed. Improvement is always needed. For example, do not be the finance manager who can only do calculations, but is unable to understand what the salespeople need. Do not be the marketing manager who knows how to prepare marketing campaigns, but does not understand tactical sales tools. Do not be the supply chain manager who looks only at saving shipment costs without understanding that you can do more business if you satisfy some customers' requests for faster shipments. Do not be the general manager who knows how to do business, but does not understand the issues that people face every day. Do not be a manager who is fully prepared in your functional area, but is unable to work with others. Working well with people is about being helpful to others, including your team members. The boss is there to serve others. The boss is not there to be served. If you adopt this mindset, you will work well with people. Who does not work well with someone who wants to help? If you have a mindset of helping others, the rest follows. You will be a good listener because you cannot help if you do not understand what people say. You will take care of people because you want to help them. When you take care of people, people will take care of you in return. You will offer direction and assign tasks, but you will not do it in a bossy way. You will assign tasks because it is part of your role — and people expect to receive direction from you. You will not give dry, top-down orders without explanations. You will explain what you ask because you want people to understand what the team needs to accomplish. You will ask for feedback and opinions. You will not be stubborn. You will welcome ideas from others. You will feel natural recognizing people's contribution and praise them. You will feel natural to be happy about people's success because you are in a mindset where them is more important than you.

People around you will feel it. If you are genuine, people will respond by helping you. It all depends on how you see yourself. If you see yourself as the top of the organization chart, you are still giving space to your ego. If you see yourself at the bottom of the organization chart, there to serve others, you will gain the hearts of others.

8.9 IT'S TIME FOR ACTION

- You need to think deeply about which roles you are currently playing, which ones are natural to you and the ones you need to put more efforts.
- How are you handling the pressure?
- Are you managing people other than completing tasks?

9

YOUR TEAM

You can achieve high performance only with a high performing team. How do you define high performing? How do you achieve high performance? Above all, *which characteristics do you want on your team*? This is a question that only you can answer — nobody else. Not even your boss can answer that question.

9.1 THE FANTASTIC FOUR

When I found my answer, everything became clear. I knew which changes I needed to apply. When you answer that last question, you know what you want. You can assess the gap, put clear steps in place, and take immediate action. I wanted in my team four key characteristics, and I called them the Fantastic Four:

- **Initiative**: my ideal team can take the initiative to solve problems and find new opportunities — without my input.
- **Accuracy**: my ideal team can deliver excellence.
- **Speed**: my ideal team can execute quickly.
- **Help**: my ideal team is helping each other. When team members help others and feel free to ask for help from others, they take appropriate actions to deliver better and faster results.

I am not sure if those Fantastic Four are universal characteristics for every team, but I am convinced that a team with those in place is high performing.

You must define your characteristics. What characteristics do you want on your team? But you cannot stop at this question. You also need to define how, when, where and to whom you will communicate those characteristics. How will you communicate? Where? When? Answer those simple questions to start filling the gaps in your team. Fifty percent of your job is defining the characteristics. The other fifty percent is living them for yourself. Be the example — and put the actions in place to make it real.

9.2 PROBLEMS OR OPPORTUNITIES?

In an ideal world, you have opportunities and no problems. In the real world, people tend to have a lot of problems. Many people oddly see opportunities as problems. The negative bias in people causes them to focus on the negative aspects. This is due to our natural survival skills. The brain easily detects what is wrong because it can be dangerous. Since good things, like opportunities, are not life-threatening, the brain does not need to focus on them. This is important for the culture of the team and the way it works. Problems and opportunities are defined by the eyes of who is looking.

Pessimistic people look at everything with black lenses. Problems are impossible to solve, problems are big, and opportunities are just another thing to work on. This negative view wastes time, resources, and energies. Optimistic people look at things with pink lenses. Problems can be solved, problems are not so big, and there is always an opportunity to do better and faster. Not much gets done when you are pessimistic or negative. If you are pessimistic in your personal life, that is your own choice, but when a manager looks at things negatively, it is another story. In the workplace, you just cannot wear black lenses all the times.

If you are optimistic and positive instead, but you let team members spread a working environment of pessimism and negativism, you are not doing a good job as a manager either. People can be as they want in their personal lives, but at work, they are paid to get results. And results get done if people have the right mindset. A positive mindset and a can-do attitude will help you and your company achieve your goals. You need to manage this aspect of yourself and your team to look at things positively and constructively. Every team has problems, and every business has problems. You need to look for solutions and learn how to grasp opportunities. You cannot allow the team to be negative or be part of the issue. You cannot confirm and reinforce the negativity. For example, customers are never fully happy. Everybody that had interactions with them knows. They often complain that you have not been fast enough, that your product or service is not good enough, that your product is too expensive, that the economy is not good enough, or that they do not have enough money to purchase. How can you and your team react to those objections? Do you think nothing can change? Do you think that customers are right when they blame your company? Then wonder why you are there. Why are you working for a company that you do not believe in?

A good manager helps the team look at things in a way that finds solutions for better business. When a customer is not satisfied, the team must find a solution. The customer will be pleased and buy more if you take care of their complaint. They will appreciate and reward you with more purchases. If you and your team react negatively — confirming that nothing can be done — you will lose the customer. They will never want to buy from a company that cannot help solve their problems.

You can use a simple matrix to plot the ideal situation and determine what you can do. If the team sees a problematic situation as an opportunity or correctly assesses an opportunity, you are in a good situation. The team will find a solution to the problem or work to get real results from a potential opportunity. If you have an opportunity, but the team looks at it negatively, they are destroying value. There is a market opportunity, but they think the company cannot do anything. This attitude will bring bad results. Nothing good will come from this thinking.

Help your team instead to work with a solution-finder mode. Help them to approach the issues rationally, with a positive mindset. Do not let negative feelings get in the way of teamwork. If the team feels that the problem has no solution, it will be like a disease: they will get sick, and nothing will be done. The more the disease spreads, the sicker the team becomes, at the point that even opportunities will be considered as negative.

You need to help the team remain in a positive state. If the team is in a negative mood, use one-on-one meetings, coaching, and development plans — or get rid of the negative team members. To reinforce good behaviors, try celebrating and praising people when the team solves a problem or transforms a problem into an opportunity

Be careful, look at your teams, observe every day, and check for negative attitudes. If negative seeds are there you need to take action.

Do not let it be. It will not resolve itself. It will only be resolved if you take action.

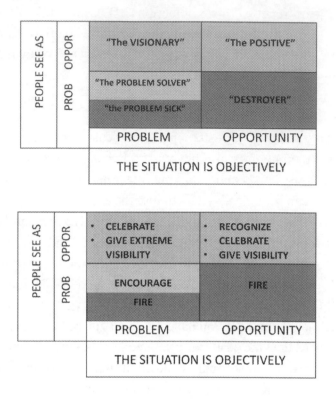

9.3 SKILLED AND WILLED

You need to assess the willpower of your employees. Are they giving the best efforts in their jobs? What level of effort do you expect from employees? You can easily assess skills, and managers are usually inclined to make skills assessments during performance reviews. In case of unsatisfactory performance, most likely, you will be required to prepare a skills-development plan.

It is much more difficult to assess the willpower of an employee. Every employee is spending the same working hours in the workplace. You might have not skilled employees who spend long hours in the office just to complete basic tasks. Spending long hours in the workplace is not an indicator of great willpower. Time is not a good KPI to assess willingness. You cannot assess willingness from their abilities or knowledge either. You might have skilled employees who are not willing to put their best effort into what they do. Willingness cannot be observed during one day or a single task. In the long term, you can notice the general attitude of an employee. Some indicators of strong willpower are:

- Willingness to do jobs not strictly related to the job description: an employee who is strict about applying their job description and making sure that all boundaries are respected does not demonstrate the best effort. I am not saying that every employee should accept whatever job or task, but when required — and if the extra task or job is an extension of their job description and the employee has the skills to do it — the employee could help. If the employee is eager to take on new jobs, new tasks, and more responsibilities and help coordinate others, it shows genuine interest.
- Willingness to offer help without being prompted: if the employee is naturally a helper, they will offer to contribute without being asked.
- Willingness to work overtime when required: I am not a supporter of overtime because if it is required regularly, it is an indicator of inefficiency and that the whole is not balanced. However, there are times when overtime is necessary. Some important jobs require a bit more time than planned, and that is not the end of the world. In those situations, employees should be ready to help.
- Willingness to do the job with excellence.
- Willingness to offer ideas and work to make them a reality.

It is important to adapt your management style to get the best from the employee. With skilled and willed people, you need to delegate. Give them autonomy. They know how to do the job and are willing to do it well. With skilled people, but little willpower, you need to find out what motivates them. Work on motivation. For employees with low skills but high willpower, you will give directions to guide them. They have the right energy, but they do not know what to do. You might give guidelines if some skills are present or clear instructions if skills are really low. For people with no skills and no willpower, you need to move them out.

Over time people change, skills are developed or lost, and people become motivated or disengaged. You cannot categorize an employee in a box and expect them to stay there forever. It is your job to motivate people to be stars. Constant observation will help you understand the best management style to apply. Do not box people into a fixed category. Every day is a good day to see improvements or regression.

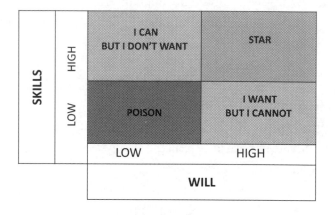

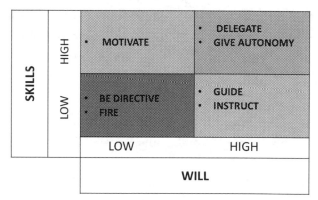

9.4 LIKE AND WILL

Can you do your best at something you do not like? During interviews, nobody told me to ask simple questions. "How much do you like your job"? Do you like what you do? Why? Do you want to continue on this career path? When you ask these questions, you can see the passion or disinterest from the interviewee. In my experience, there are high chances that people who like what they do will also be good performers.

However, liking a job does not mean that people will put in the effort. I would like to have a fit body, but I do not put in the effort with exercise and diet. The same happens on the job. Some people would like to be managers, for example, because of the higher salaries and benefits, but how many of them will put effort into being prepared to be great managers?

You can see it in a matrix.

- People who like the job and put in the effort. This is the best category. They will put their best efforts, in the short and long-term, and they will try to overachieve. They are motivated to do it because they like it. You are lucky if you have them on your team. You can count on them. It is your responsibility to keep them motivated and help them achieve their dreams.

- People who like what they do but are not committed to putting in the effort: They will probably swing between good and not-so-good results. They will have some good results in the short term, but they will not be determined to persist. In stressful situations, they give up easily. You have to monitor their efforts and discipline. You have to make sure the job is done. When delegating, you have to stay informed on developments, or you risk a poor job or a late delivery.

- People who do not like what they do but are willing to put in the effort: they might do the job for example because they have been prompted by their family's needs or wishes even if the job is not their real passion. They could have chosen the job

131

because they needed the salary. Since they put in the effort, they are responsible, accountable, and they know what they are supposed to do. You can count on them, but the fact that they do not like what they do will probably affect the quality of their work. It might not always be excellent. In this case, you need to recognize their efforts. It is best if you can help them change their perspective and be happier with what they do.

- People who do not like what they do and are not willing to put in the effort: They do not have the interest at all and will not do well. They will be apathetic at work. They will not spread positive energy. You need to watch out. They will spread poison or drain positive energy from the organization. It is better to get rid of this kind of employee as soon as possible. You must control their behavior. Do not let them set a bad example for others.

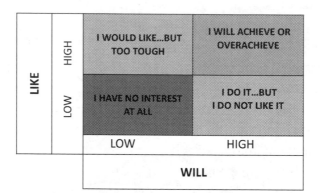

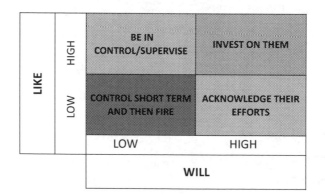

9.5 ALTRUISTIC AND SELFISH

Another element to be aware of is the attitude toward others. Some people are selfish, and others are altruistic. Selfishness and altruism are absolute opposites. The people who perform better in a company are altruistic, at least in the medium-long term. Working as a real team, with high performing teamwork, is critical for the success of any business. People who are genuinely altruistic tend to do better at teamwork. They will help others naturally and receive help when they are in need. People like them, and this helps them be seen favorably. Selfish people will not be liked. They will take care only of themselves without taking care of others.

This is another aspect that business schools and companies do not teach. In any company, there will be a mix of people. If managers start to consider, consciously, and intentionally, this characteristic, more people will fit the values of the company.

Behind teamwork, there is altruism. You can start to scout for this characteristic since the recruiting phase. In interviews, the candidate displays their willingness to help others. Specific questions can assess this characteristic. I always try to hire people who are naturally altruistic. I have been lucky to work with selfish people, and I have seen the negative effect on the organization. They were not approached by other colleagues for help. They were alone at their desks and didn't interact with others. They were not available for anything and anyone. When those people are smart, they believe that everyone else is stupid — and they treat others as useless. They will not listen to other opinions, and sooner or later, they will bully others.

It is important to understand a second aspect: if people are dominant/extroverts or submissive/introverts. There is nothing bad about being one extreme, but there can be problems when you combine them with selfishness. Selfishness is not a good characteristic for a team. It never helps an organization.

As a manager, you will encounter two types of people to be on guard:

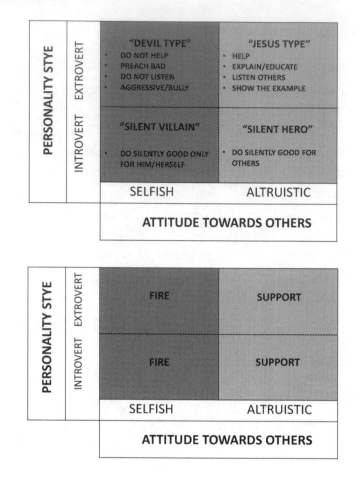

9.5.1 The Devil Type

They are selfish and dominant/extrovert. When they achieve results, it will be hard for you to decide to fire them. However, it is the right thing to do. In the long term, those people will be bad for your organization. They can help you achieve short-term results, but the costs will be high. Your organization will never grow as a team. Results will be linked to that person, and businesses cannot rely on a few egocentric, selfish people. These people will never be able to build a culture of teamwork. You might have short-term results, but you will never have a team nor long-term performance.

9.5.2 The Silent Villain

These people are difficult to spot. They are silent, sit at their desks, do not bully others, are not visibly aggressive, and do not have highly visible negative behaviors. It is like a drop of poison every day — it will kill your team slowly. It is important to observe your team members constantly. For sure, 360-degree assessments are useful for spotting people who are not helping others. You can get a lot of feedback from other team members. You can also notice the relationships they build on the team. There will be some conflicts with this team member, and people will not count on their help.

9.6 ZEROS, ONES, AND INFINITE TYPES

I try to surround myself with the right newcomers, team members, colleagues, and hopefully bosses too:

- those who have the fantastic four characteristics (initiative, accuracy, speed, help others)
- those who see opportunities
- those who find solutions to problems
- those who have strong willpower
- those who are skilled or are willing to learn and develop skills
- those who like their jobs
- those who are willing to help others

I try to minimize the presence of those who are the opposite, and I try to change their negative characteristics:

- those who do not have the fantastic four characteristics
- those who only see problems without proposing solutions
- those who never see opportunities
- those who are lazy and lack determination and commitment
- those who have no skills or are not willing to develop them

- those who do not like what they do
- those who are selfish and never help others

If the working environment you build is positive, a majority of people will fall into the first category: the right people. If the working environment you build is not positive instead, people will not perform. You will have the wrong people with you. It seems to be a chicken-and-egg dilemma. Do you need the right people to build a performing working environment — or the right environment to have performing people? It is probably a mix of the two, and you need to work on both aspects: build the conditions to help people succeed and pick the right people to help you and the organization perform. People can decide who they want to be in the workplace:

- Zeros are destroyers: they destroy value.
- Ones are neutral: they keep the value as it is.
- Infinity types: they grow the value of others.

If you have a team of four people, one might be a bad team member (a zero). This negative team player will destroy the value of the others. If you have four people, and all four are "one" type, you will keep the value as it is.

If you have four "infinite" type on your team, they multiply the value of the others. They multiply the value of the entire team. Those people are the stars who have all positive characteristics. Look at the matrices and quadrants from the previous chapters. The best people are helping others grow and are helping the team perform. The key characteristic of the infinite type is an inner willingness to help others. Those people will do their best and improve their weaknesses because they want to help.

Not everyone is born as "infinite" type. It is a choice that people can consciously and intentionally make. We are not trained to know that we can decide who we want to be. A majority of people wrongly believe they are who they are for the rest of their life. Those people believe, for example, in having a fixed amount of intelligence, so if they are not smart, they will never be smarter. If they do not have analytical skills or are not good with numbers, they will never be. If they are not good at public speaking, they will never be. If they do not know how to sell, they never will.

A majority of people wrongly believe and rely only on nature and natural talent. They believe you are what nature gave you. Few people believe in nurture, which is the possibility to develop. In her book, *Mindset,* Dr. Carol S. Dweck talks about "fixed" and "growth" mindsets (Dweck, 2017). In a fixed mindset, there is nothing that can change. In the growth mindset, people think they can develop.

I believe in a combination of nature and nurture and in a combination of fixed and growth mindsets. People are born with some natural talents, but if they are not trained, they will be lost. People without unique talents instead can become good at something — maybe not excellent, but good, putting the right smart effort.

People can choose who they want to be. In the workplace, people can choose to be destroyers, neutral, or infinite types. Infinite does not mean being the manager, director, or CEO. Everyone, in every role and position, can be infinite type by doing its best and being open to help others to become better.

Imagine an entry-level accountant who is working accurately, matching deadlines, showing to the finance manager issues he cannot solve alone, asking for advice, sending required reports to colleagues, always being correct and on time, trying to explain how accounting works to nonfinancial specialists and being open to suggestions from colleagues or the boss for how to improve the reports. This is an infinite team member. The same person, in the same role, can decide to act differently: submitting jobs with mistakes, being late, staying silent when problems arise, not sending updates to colleagues, thinking that others do not understand accounting. This person is a destroyer.

A majority of people are neutral. They do their jobs, but they do not think they can contribute to the team's success. They are not of the mindset to help their colleagues achieve more and do better than yesterday.

Your team has people from all three categories. If you want a high-performing team, it is your job to keep neutral people — or help them become infinite people — support the infinite people and let go of the zero types. A Gauss curve explains the state you should find in the workplace (in the absence of managerial intervention): a few infinite types, a few destroyers, and a majority of neutral types.

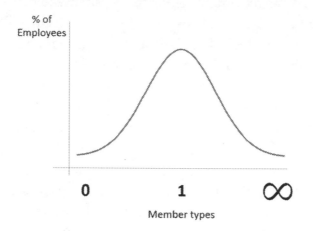

You can change this distribution by actively working on people and the working environment. The more infinite types you have, the better. The fewer zeros, the better. If you put a real action plan in place, you can have a different team.

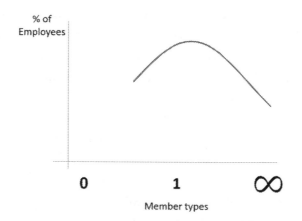

Achieving this state is not easy. It takes a lot of effort. It takes working on every detail of the rational and emotional parts. It takes daily attention. It does not come just by luck. If you achieve this state, do not think your job is over. If you do not nurture it every day, it will go back to the initial state. If you work for this stage, you will see results. Your team will achieve higher and higher. You will be surprised to see how much happens without your intervention. You will be amazed to see what others can do. It depends a lot on you. You have to put all the rational parts in place, be clear on your role, pick the right people, develop them, and work with them to have a great workplace.

People can decide which type they want to be. You will have some difficult people, but they have the choice to change. You can ask, "Who do you want to be? Someone who wants to help the team to grow or fail? Do you want to be a zero, a one, or an infinite?"

If there is no change, make clear to the employee that there is no space for zero types. At last, who are you? Among managers, there are zero types as well. Are you one of them? Are you helping your team grow? If not, you are not a good manager. You can change what you do every day. Just try to help others do a better job. Do your best — to the best of your abilities — improve yourself every day, and constantly ask if you are doing your best to help others succeed. The key is others. If they succeed, you succeed. Success is not only about you. If you are the manager, improve yourself first — and then help others to improve. Do not think others are the only ones who must improve.

9.7 ARE THEY SATISFIED?

You always have to make sure your team is keen on improving. Every day, it is possible to do something better, faster, or more efficiently. Improvement is constant, never-ending. Many people do not like change. Many prefer the comfortable familiarity of what they currently do.

When your team does not see the need to improve, that is a worrying bad sign. It means they are satisfied with the current results. It means the team performance will decline sooner or later because a competitor is already improving, while you do not. When a team feels satisfied, it will lose the energy to do well. They will think more about how to improve their personal lives — maybe work less, maybe get a higher salary, maybe have more holidays — rather than how to do good for the company or their department.

When team members care only about themselves, they work less, they do not improve, and they lose focus. Performance starts to decline. The company does not achieve great results; it stalls and then fall. The company cannot pay bonuses and salary increases, and the people are not satisfied. Unsatisfied people leave the company. A vicious cycle has begun with a feeling of satisfaction.

If the team never feels satisfied, instead, it knows that improvement is always possible. They try to do things better or faster or more efficiently. They try new things. If they are not satisfied, they will end up with more benefits as they will work more, they will be more focused, their performance will improve, the company will improve and grow, and the company could pay bonuses and salary increases. When people are satisfied, new people will be hired to fuel growth. A virtuous cycle has begun with a feeling of dissatisfaction.

The key point is, satisfaction or not, about the current situation. When teams and team members do not see the need for improvement, alarms should go off in your head. It is important to have happy people — but not satisfied people. You need to have people who constantly seek improvements.

Everything starts with you. Are you satisfied? Are you looking for improvements? Are you asking for improvements from your teams? The perfect world does not exist. There is always something that can be done better. If you think everything is good and nothing must be improved, you are wrong. Your mindset is a big part of your team's performance. If you think that it is okay and no improvements are needed, the performance will never improve — and it will start to decline. If you think there is always something that can be done better, it will. Everything is in your head. If you feel disconnected from the team because you are not satisfied and they are, do not worry. You are right.

Only actions generate results. If your team is satisfied, and there is no urgency to improve, actions will not be triggered. Keep an eye on the sense of satisfaction of your team. It is good when people are happy only when the results are good or great, or progress is steady and vigorous. However, even when the team achieves good results, you cannot allow the team to relax. It is your responsibility to find new ways to motivate people to further improve.

I was speaking to someone in the organization about our sales growth. Sales were growing quickly, around 30 percent per year, and expectations were high. A team member said, "Boss, why isn't 5 percent growth enough?" That was a big alert for me. Knowing that people thought we should be happy about such little growth scared me. I started to talk more about our objectives and why we should aim higher. As a result, the team was in a constant search for improvements, and performance continued to soar.

You will have different people on the team, and their perceptions about change will be different. You will have four basic kinds of people:

- People who are happy with changes. They see the change as positive and take action.
- People who know that change is inevitable, but they are not willing to change their habits.
- People who are happy with the current reality and do not want to change.
- People who are not happy with the current reality, but they do not want to change. They blame their current reality, but they are not working actively for improvement.

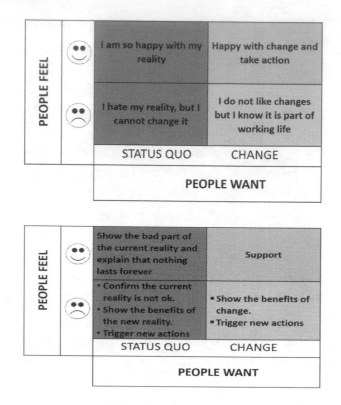

Everything will change over time — for the better or the worse — and it depends on which values the team and team members embrace. Some values are good, and others are bad. People who strive for simplicity, speed, optimism, energy, accuracy, punctuality, openness, and helping others will bring positive changes. Complex, slow, pessimistic, unenergetic, inaccurate, late, close, and selfish people will generate a bad future. When you have people with positive values, you have people who are helping you today, and they will also build a good future for the organization — with or without you as the manager. When you have people with negative values instead, they are not helping you today and they will also poison the company and hamper its future. Having the right people is a vital requirement for the present and the future.

Strong people display behaviors that represent their values. They are fast, energetic, and optimistic. They inspire others and are examples to others. The same strength can be used for negative values. Negative people gossip, blame others, are pessimistic, come late to meetings, are not open to suggestions, and bully others.

You have superheroes and villains in every story — and every company, including yours. Try to add a lot of good people and minimize the bad ones in your team. Their strength level can be high or low. Some people show their values with less strength: they do not speak or act loudly.

In the end, every person is an agent of change. Every person represents positive or negative changes and positive or negative strengths. There should not be place in an organization for people with negative values. The solution is getting them off of your team. It is easy to spot the destroyers, but more difficult to catch the silent poison agents as constant observation is required.

Firing people is not easy, but it must be done when people are not helping to build a good future. Assess the values your team members represent and make your decision. It can be difficult when bad people are bringing good results. Results are short term, but values last forever. Do not keep bad people because of the results they bring. You can enjoy short-term results, but sooner or later, you will regret having them on your team. You will never enjoy the journey if you have bad people around you. However, it is not only about you. Bad people will not build a good environment for others too.

When you have bad apples in the basket, it is never good.

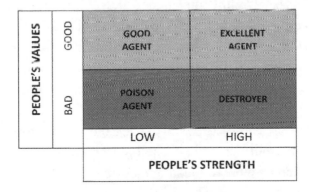

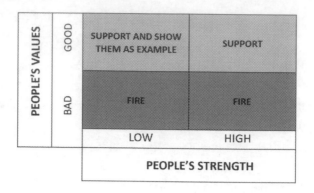

9.8 PAIN AND PLEASURE

People do what they do because they want to feel pleasure or avoid pain. They want to gain something or avoid losing something. They want to have a reward or avoid a punishment.

I learned a fundamental lesson that is critical for being a good manager. In the beginning, I thought everything could be achieved through logical discussions. I thought it was enough to present a logical proposal to show customers the win-win result. With my team, I thought it was enough to agree on the end goal. I was a firm believer that I could overcome all issues with logic, but I was wrong. Logic can help a lot with the big picture and finding a rational solution to a problem. I still use logic and a rational approach with myself. However, when sharing, discussing, or communicating with the external world, I understood that things get done through the combination of pain and pleasure or fear and joy. Those two *proto-emotions* are the earliest forms of emotions (Vallverdú, 2017). Psychologists refer to them as *seed emotions* since all other emotions grow from those two basic forms. When I discovered proto-emotions, I found a framework for my experience.

I learned the importance of being flexible in moving from pain to pleasure or from fear to joy. The biggest lesson has been with a specific customer with serious payment issues. With the sales and finance team, we were trying to find solutions to the issue. We tried the logical, rational approach, which has always been my natural setting. We met the customer to explain the payment discrepancies. We thought our logical point of view would be enough to close the issue. We thought the situation was simple to explain and simple to agree on: they bought products from us, and we expected the payment in return. We listened at the customer's perspective about why the payments were not made. They did not use a logical approach. They put so many excuses on the table that I could not believe what they were saying. They were referring to past promises from previous sales managers — from two or three years before — or that customers, like them, should be entitled to having suppliers satisfy all their requests. They argued that other companies were always agreeing with them. There was no logic at all.

We tried to explain that we had a contract with clear terms and expected the payment based on the contract. The struggle continued for a couple of years. We were speaking logically, and they were not speaking logically. I learned that logic could not fight non-logic.

In the end, we tried to negotiate to give in in some requests and to inform them about punishments that would come in the case of no payment. It was a combination of offering good benefits and showing potential penalties. We provided some extra discounts to close the issue, and we introduced discount cuts in case of payment delays. In the end, it worked. With that customer, I could not use my preferred way (the pleasure way). Sometimes you have to switch to pain mode. Lesson learned: it is best when you can fluently move between the two, reward and punishment, joy and fear, pleasure and pain.

This also applies to your people. Some people are motivated because they want pleasure or want to avoid pain. You can also call it the stick-and-carrot method. You will have a natural preference for one of the two, but you will perform at your best when you learn to utilize both. For example, on your team, you will have people who are motivated because they want to do well for themselves or want to achieve a bonus, a salary increase, or a good career. These people work for pleasure, and you need to manage them by offering what they need. Other people work because you constantly supervise them. If they do not achieve the target, they will lose the bonus, miss a salary increase, have a negative performance review, or hear negative feedback in front of others. These people are motivated by avoiding pain.

Some people will be motivated by pleasure: "Dear Joe, let's achieve this goal. By doing so, you will get a bonus." "Dear Joe, let's achieve this goal. By doing so, you will be in a good position for your next career move."

Others will work only to avoid pain: "Dear Joe, come to my office tomorrow and show me the progress." "Dear Joe, if this job is not done by Friday, you will have to finish this weekend." To customers, it will sound different, but the point is the same: "Dear customer, let's achieve this goal together. By doing so, you will get my company to support you with a good marketing campaign", or "Dear customer, if you do not achieve this goal, you will lose your current discount."

At the beginning of my experience as a manager, I was only in one mode: pleasure, joy, reward, carrot. In the end, that is what motivates me. I work for myself, for my self-realization, and my pleasure. I never worked because someone told me to do so. However, it is not the same for everyone. You need to understand your preferred mode and practice the other one when it is appropriate.

Management has to move from one position to another. Management has to move from the starting point to another stage. I always talk about moving from A, where we are now, to B, where we will be tomorrow. Moving from A to B can be done in many ways by combining the two opposite approaches.

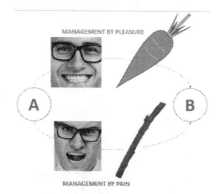

You can remind yourself about what you have to do:

- You need to know from where you start. What is the starting point? What are you not satisfied with? What do you need to change?
- You need to know where you want to land. How does it look at the end? What is your objective?
- Which way do you want to take? Management by pleasure or management by pain?
- Once you decide on the way, follow it. Do not doubt yourself wondering, "What if I had chosen a different path?" You made your choice — and you cannot go back in time. Go ahead. You can decide to change your path in the future, but do not moan about what you could have done.

Pleasure Tools	Pain Tools
share and agree on vision and goals	supervision
set bonuses based on targets	micromanagement
celebrate successes	frequent reviews
team-building activities	tough performance reviews
clear job descriptions	working long hours
help building processes	not help to build processes
help to solve problems	not help to solve problems
help in any form	no help
encouragement	negative feedback
recognition	publicly showing others the bad results
salary increase	no salary increases

You have to make many decisions every day and will constantly define the path you want to take. Only choosing one way is not good. Only choosing pleasure or only pain will not bring you to a successful state. It can be difficult to move away from your natural preference, but with a self-conscious effort, you can do it. Do not be the manager who is always managing by pleasure, joy, gain, or reward. There are occasions when you cannot manage in that way.

However, do not be the manager who always manages by fear.

Make a conscious effort to understand the best approach for every situation. You will find that you need to move between the two. I do not think the perfect ratio exists for how much pleasure or pain you should use. It depends on the situation.

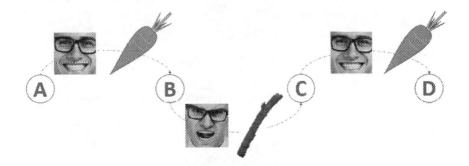

After four years of managing the same company, I was pretty happy with the processes, teams, and customer relationships, allowing me to go back to my ideal and preferred style of management by pleasure. In the past, I would have done better by using a bit more management by pain.

9.9 IT'S TIME FOR ACTION

- Which ideal characteristics do you want in your team? Which gaps do you observe? What is your plan to get what you want?
- Is your team effectively finding solutions to problems and grasping opportunities?
- Are your team members skilled?
- Do your team members like their jobs?
- Are they willing to put efforts?
- Do you have unhealthy selfish people in your team? What is your plan for them?
- Which are your best team members that are helping others to grow? Are you supporting them?
- Is your team already satisfied? How do you keep them motivated to continue to innovate?
- Are you managing by pain and by pleasure, depending on the situation?

10

A SUCCESSFUL ORGANIZATION

W hat are the elements of a successful organization?

10.1 FROM STRATEGY TO ATTITUDE

When I was younger, I thought you could succeed if you had a great strategy. I thought this was true in business and other aspects of life. At school, if you have a good method for studying, a good grade is guaranteed. If you have a good training plan and good exercise, you will be fit. I always believed in having a good plan. I was fifty percent right.

Without a plan, you will not do well — unless you have good luck. You need another ingredient for success: attitude. This is valid for you, for all the people you manage, and for the overall organization. What is your attitude? What is the attitude of your team?

Attitude is the basic element for your team's success. Time is the only dimension you cannot influence. You cannot speed it up, and you cannot slow it down. Look at the time as the number of possible changes. How many changes can you do in a certain time unit? If you look at the year, one year equals one change and so on:

- 1 year = 1 change per year
- 12 months = 12 changes per year
- 52 weeks = 52 changes per year
- 365 days = 365 changes per year
- 8,760 hours = 8,760 changes per year
- 525,600 minutes = 525,600 changes per year
- 31,536,000 seconds = 31,536,000 changes per year

It all depends on how you look at time. If you decide to look at time with a big horizon, like a year, you will be stuck thinking you can only have one change. If you only look at time in term of a year, you risk looking in absolute terms: "a good year" or "a bad year." If you look at time in months, you can be more positive since you will have twelve opportunities. The magic is when you see time in days or hours: "What can I do today to be better than yesterday? What can I do during this hour to make my day?" You will see time as a great opportunity. You will even feel an abundance of time.

When you look at business strategy, the time horizon is long. If the organization wants to achieve something in the next ten years, it can be broken down into five- or three-year plans. The base unit of strategy in business is typically one year, the budget for next year.

In the budget, you will have strategic pillars for the following year. You will have good or bad assumptions for the coming year, and that is your strategy. You might be part of the definition of the strategy. You could have a say or not, but you will have one strategy. If you or your company are changing strategies in less than a year, there is confusion, which means the goal is not clear.

With a monthly action plan, you and your team will do real actions every day, and those actions can be split into tasks and subtasks for every hour. From strategy to subtasks, the time horizon is from the year to the hour. You and your team must also truly *care* about what you are doing. What should you and your team do every minute to be successful? What do you and your team do every second? That is attitude, that is about beliefs and values. That is who you and your teams are and truly stand for.

You must learn how to master your rational tools. Those tools will help you prepare the strategy and action plan and make sure actions are happening through tasks and subtasks. If you stop there, you can only control fifty percent of what your team is doing. The other fifty percent is the emotional part. Does your team care about what they are doing? What is their attitude? Are they engaged? Are they working because someone told them to or because that is what they want?

You cannot only look for people who are skilled at their jobs. You need much more. You need people who are motivated inside, who have willpower, who see problems as opportunities, who are altruists, and who help others grow. The same applies to you. You can be skilled, but you also need to have all the other characteristics. If you want to be a great manager, you need to care about what you do. Are you helping others? Are you selfish? Do you work to make your ego bigger? If you believe in your heart that you are there to help others succeed, you will be a great manager.

Last, but not least: everything starts with you and within you. To be a great manager is essential you understand yourself and know how to manage yourself. Manage yourself before you manage others. Do not think that your role is only to manage others. You are the first one to be managed. You are your first subordinate. So, ask yourself if you have the right attitude.

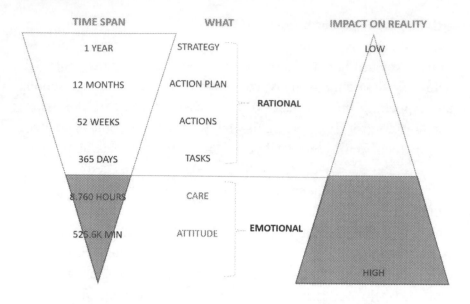

10.2 FORMULA FOR SUCCESS

To have a successful organization, you need to take care of your people, but first of all, you must ask them to deliver. It is a balance between what you offer people (give) and what you ask of them (take). Look at what you give them, how you take care of them and at the results and behaviors you demand. Do you care about your people? Are you demanding?

My formula for success is simple:

SUCCESS = DEMANDING + CARING

Demanding (TAKE)	Caring (GIVE)
results-oriented	offer help
behaviors	give face
discipline	recognition
accuracy	respect
speed	ask for opinions
commitment	celebrate
openness	say thank you
respect	explain
cooperation	explain again, repeat
solve problems	forgive
invent and find new opportunities	give benefits

You need to keep both aspects in balance. If you only take care of people, your organization will be spoiled — but there will not be positive tension towards results. If you are merely demanding, you might achieve short-term results, but it will not be sustainable long term. Sooner or later, people will leave.

I have been lucky to see two kinds of managers at work: those who believe in people and those who do not. In 1960, Douglas McGregor introduced theory X and theory Y (MindTools.com). Managers X type believe people are not inclined to give their best at work, prefer to be lazy, and work as little as possible. They do not have ambitions and work just to pay the bills. There is a base disbelief in people. On the contrary, managers Y type trust that people are motivated in their jobs, are self-directed to give their best and don't need constant supervision. Managers Y believe in people.

I realized that the manager best performs combining the two extreme aspects of Douglas McGregor's theory. Blending the manager X and Y, creating a new type: the manager Z type. I believe in people so that I would be a manager Y according to the theory. But I am not naïve enough to think you can trust everyone. Once you pick the right people, you can trust them. Or you can trust people that demonstrated to be trustworthy. According to the theory, I would be a manger X, but also Y. That's why I think of myself as a manager Z type, the one that combines both aspects.

When you trust people, automatically, your behaviors are friendly. Your influencing style will be positive. You will not use authority to impose your ideas, and you will include people in discussions. You will use an inclusive management style. You will naturally praise people. You will work with others as partners. You will see your people — even subordinates — as colleagues. In the end, you are one of them. You are part of the same team. You will not feel superior — even if your organization chart says so.

Combining the formula for success (caring and demanding) and manager type X (positive influence style) or Y (negative influence style), I came up with the below seven types of organization.

10.2.1 The A-Team

It consists of caring and demanding cultures where the manager is a type Y (believes people are self-motivated). In this type of organization, the manager has a positive influencing style and believes in their people. The manager is taking care of their people and has high expectations for results and behaviors. People will feel important, respected, and engaged, and they will deliver what is asked of them. In this situation, the team will feel united, motivated, and inspired. The team members are there with their minds and their hearts.

10.2.2 B-Team (Group of soldiers)

It consists of caring and demanding cultures where the manger is a type X (believes people requires supervision). This team will achieve results and will be disciplined. There will be no execution problems, at least for the short or medium term, but the emotional ingredient of unity will not be there. People will not feel engaged with the manager. If the manager does not believe in their people, why should people believe in their manager? This efficient group of people — or soldiers — will say yes to the authoritative style of the manager, but they will not be there for long. How could a manager X truly and deeply take care of people? That is still possible, in the short and medium-term, by implementing a good reward system. However, that manager will probably lack intangible and emotional rewards, making the team members not fully engaged. Team members are there with their minds, but not with their hearts.

10.2.3 C-Team (Group of people)

When you have a demanding manager with a positive influencing style but with no true care for people, you will see a group of people working independently and maybe delivering short-term results. In the long term, people will feel a lack of real caring. The manager can be nice and polite with people in the short term, but without truly taking care of them, it is a matter of time before people stop giving their best.

10.2.4 D-Team (Stressed individuals)

When the manager is demanding, not caring, and uses a negative influencing style. People will be stressed for short-term results. People will work independently, without building a real team, and lack of common goals. There will be a lot of conflicts. Results could be achieved short term, but people will be squeezed and so stressed out. That is not a sustainable situation.

10.2.5 E-Team (Happy spoiled employees)

When the manager is not demanding but is taking care of people with a positive influencing style. The organization will be lazy, spoiled, and loose. Nothing will be achieved.

10.2.6 F-Team (Unhappy spoiled employees)

When the manager is not demanding but is caring, and the management style is negative. You will see lazy and spoiled employees who are against the company. There will be a lot of conflicts.

10.2.7 Z-Team (Nothing)

When the manager is not demanding, is not caring, and uses a negative influencing style. You have nothing. There is no team, and there is no group. It is a horrible situation where the manager can treat the employees badly.

	A-Team	Group of Soldiers	Group of People	Stressed Individuals	Happy Spoiled employees	Unhappy Spoiled employees
DEMANDING	YES	YES	YES	YES	NO	NO
CARING	YES	YES	NO	NO	YES	YES
INFLUENCING STYLE	POSITIVE	NEGATIVE	POSITIVE	NEGATIVE	POSITIVE	NEGATIVE
RESULT	THE UNITED TEAM YOU WANT	Efficient group of disciplined people	Motivated group of people for short term	Stressed people to achieve short terms results	Spoiled and lazy employees waiting for the next reward	Spoiled and lazy employees against the manager
STATUS SHORT TERM	OK	OK	OK	SO-SO	NOT OK	NOT OK
STATUS LONG TERM	OK	SO-SO	NOT OK	NOT OK	NOT OK	NOT OK

10.2.8 Consequences of the Formula for Success

We can make some considerations:

- First, to have a successful organization, you must be demanding. If you do not have challenging goals to achieve, the organization will be lazy. Never lower your standards.
- Second, if you take care of people without being demanding, you are building spoiled employees. Do not think that only taking care of people is enough to be successful. If you take care of people, they will love you — but you are not going to achieve results. The company will fire you.
- Third, in the short term, you can be successful as a manager without truly taking care of people. In the short term, you can achieve results just by being demanding. Still, it is better in the short term if you have a positive influencing style.
- Fourth, in the long term, you both need to be demanding and take care of people. It is better if your influencing style is also positive.

When you start managing, you might not have ever asked before to people to do things. You might not know how to ask. You risk not being demanding. You might feel better not asking others and doing things by yourself. That is not sustainable for you or your team. Being a manager does not mean to please people. Just being nice with your people does not make you a good manager. Listening only to your people's needs is not what you must do.

You can take care of people and listen to their needs, still being demanding. You can look at being demanding as your ability to listen to the needs of your company. Try to balance the two perspectives: your people and your company. Do not take only one side. You need to manage both sides. It is not easy — but that is why not everyone is the manager. And that is why not every manager is a good one.

10.3 MY SELF-ASSESSMENT

What I want from my ideal organization does not matter for you. What matters is what you want. You are the manager, and you will manage. You will find many people around who would like to help you with advice, techniques, experiences to share, books to read, and podcasts to listen to. Getting help from people is important, but in the end, you decide how to manage. You will find your management style based on what you believe.

Reflect on what you want from your organization and your team. What do you want? The answer to this question will influence your management style. When you write it down and clearly express what you want, you can put in place a conscious and intentional plan to make it happen. That will affect your management style. You will achieve what you want — or be close to, if you are clear about what you want, have a plan, and measure your progress.

Below my self-assessment.

What kind of organization do I want? "A data-driven, scientific organization that can achieve results based on analysis and a rational approach to the business, where plans and measurement is the key."

What kind of people do I want around me? "Positive, analytic, logic, open to the new, accurate, ready to help others, take the initiative, able to get negative feedback without getting offended, simple, energetic, fast, disciplined, on time, open to giving feedback."

What kind of processes do I want? "Automated, detailed, stable, easy-to-delegate processes that can become routine as soon as possible."

What kind of systems do I want? "One system — from where people can pull whatever information they need."

What kind of execution do I want? "Accurate, fast, smooth, simple, coordinated among departments, planned."

Knowing what you want is important, but knowing what you do not want is important too. If knowing what you want is driving you to that destination, knowing what you do not want will help you avoid being distracted along the way. By defining what you do not want, you will know if you are where you do not want to go. So, be clear about what you do not want too.

What kind of organization do I not want? "Pure relationship and gut feeling."

What kind of people do I not want around you? "Negative, illogical, confused, close to the new, stubborn, not careful, selfish, unreliable, take negative feedbacks as personal attacks, late, not available to give feedback to others, complex, passive."

What kind of systems do I not want? "Too many different data sources."

What kind of execution do I not want? "Inaccurate, slow, complicated, complex, unplanned."

What are the gaps between what I want and where I am? What are the elements that I do not want that are instead present? Those are the questions that triggered my corrective actions.

- Gaps in Organization: not enough "data-ability." This is how I define the capability of employees to manage data in spreadsheets — the ability to drag conclusions from data.
- Gaps in People: some negativism, not analytical enough, not enough discipline, not ready to give feedback, not accurate enough, slow, passive.

Below the actions I took to address the gaps:

Gap	Actions	Next Immediate Action
some negativism	recognize individual/team achievements more and celebrate them more	▪ tell x how good he is doing ▪ ask x to do the same with their team
not analytical enough	prepare standard and automated reporting	▪ prepare a new report ▪ schedule a recurring weekly meeting to read the numbers with sales and marketing
not disciplined enough	train on Microsoft Outlook and enforce on-time/accuracy	▪ ask managers to learn and coach their teams ▪ send a tutorial to all
not ready to give feedback	plan scheduled one-on-one meetings and team meetings	▪ ask managers to schedule monthly team meetings ▪ prepare a structured template for a one-on-one meeting to use across teams ▪ ask managers to send feedback after one-on-one meetings

not accurate enough	structure templates to follow and discuss when not okay	<ul><li>speak out when I am not satisfied with the result</li><li>ask managers to prepare templates</li><li>help structuring templates</li></ul>
slow (from idea to action)	better minutes templates with clear deadlines, owners, and follow-through tracking	<ul><li>close every meeting with a minute of the meeting and start the following meeting with a revision of the previous minutes</li></ul>
passive	ask for more involvement during the planning phase	<ul><li>ask managers to prepare timelines on projects and ask them to schedule recurring meetings as checkpoint</li></ul>

Since I found the time to define these actions clearly, my organization started to change. The progress has been so rewarding. At the end of the process, I had the best team I could dream of. A long time ago, I thought too many things were not in place to succeed, but I was wrong. I had to define what I wanted, clearly understand the gap, and take actions to correct them. All managers have the same problem — not everything around us is exactly as we would like to be. You can take your given situation as unchangeable and live a life of complaint, or, think you are the one who can change it. It will not happen overnight, but it will change. You will feel good, and you will see progress. Start the journey. Start changing to get what you want. Now it is your turn.

10.4 IT'S TIME FOR ACTION

What kind of organization do you want?

_____

_____

_____

_____

What kind of people do you want in your team?

_____

_____

_____

_____

What kind of processes do you want?

_____

_____

_____

_____

What kind of systems do you want?

_____

_____

_____

_____

What kind of execution do you want?

_____

_____

_____

_____

What kind of organization do you not want?

_____

_____

_____

_____

What kind of people do you not want in your team?

_____

_____

_____

_____

What kind of processes do you not want?

_____

_____

_____

_____

What kind of systems do you not want?

_____

_____

_____

_____

What kind of execution do you not want?

_____

_____

_____

_____

Which Gaps do you have today?

Area	Gap
goals	
organization	
people	
processes	
systems	
execution	
innovation	

Which Actions are required?

Area	Gap	Action
goals		
organization		
people		
processes		
systems		
execution		
innovation		

Which Next Immediate Action can you take by tomorrow?

Area	Gap	Action	Next Immediate Action
goals			
organization			
people			
processes			
systems			
execution			
innovation			

11

LEADERSHIP AND MANAGEMENT

These pragmatic quotes about leadership and management inspired my management style and might also help you to define yours. What are your takeaways after reading these quotes?

Quote	My takeaways
Leadership is the capacity to translate vision into reality. –Warren Bennis	From idea to action.
Leaders think and talk about the solutions. Followers think and talk about the problems. –Brian Tracy	Solutions, not problems.
The leader has to be practical and a realist yet must talk the language of the visionary and the idealist. –Eric Hoffer	Be pragmatic, but express the idea.
Logic will get you from A to B. Imagination will take you everywhere. –Albert Einstein	Logic yes, but more imagination.

He who has learned how to obey will know how to command. –Solon	Discipline.
Leadership is the art of getting someone else to do something you want done because he wants to do it. –General Dwight Eisenhower	Influence without order.
Before you are a leader, success is all about growing yourself. When you become leader, success is all about growing others. –Jack Welch	Grow others.
The art of leadership is saying no, not saying yes. It is very easy to say yes. –Tony Blair	When necessary, say no.
I start with the premise that the function of leadership is to produce more leaders, not more followers. –Ralph Nader	Produce more leaders.
A great person attracts great people and knows how to hold them together. –Johann Wolfgang Von Goethe	Attract and hold great people.
If your actions inspire others to dream more, learn more, do more and become more, you are a leader. –John Quincy Adams	Inspire others to do more.

Anyone can hold the helm when the sea is calm. –Publilius Syrus	Drive in difficult situations.
A good general not only sees the way to victory; he also knows when victory is impossible. –Polybius	Assess what and when not possible.
You don't have to hold a position in order to be a leader. –Henry Ford	Influence without authority.
It is better to lead from behind and to put others in front, especially when you celebrate victory when nice things occur. You take the front line when there is danger. Then people will appreciate your leadership. –Nelson Mandela	Give credit to others.
Management is doing things right; leadership is doing the right thing. –Peter Drucker	Know what to do and how.
A leader is best when people barely know he exists, when his work is done, his aim fulfilled, they will say: we did it ourselves. –Lao Tzu	Make others successful.
The best executive has sense to pick good men to do what he wants done, and self-restraint to keep from meddling with them while they do it. –Theodore Roosevelt	Pick the right people and let them do.

Never tell people how to do things. Tell them what to do and they will surprise you with their ingenuity. –General George Patton	Give clear direction, not orders.
If you cannot do great things, do small things in a great way. –Napoleon Hill	Do everything great.
Leadership and learning and indispensable to each other. –John F. Kennedy	Continuous learning.
There are four ingredients in true leadership: brains, souls, heart, and good nerves. –Klaus Schwab	Rational and emotional, and keep calm.
A leader is one who knows the way, goes the way and show the way. –John Maxwell	Know, do and show.
Great leaders are not defined by absence of weakness, but rather by the presence of clear strengths. –John Zenger	Push on strengths.
Success is walking from failure to failure with no loss of enthusiasm. –Winston Churchill	Show enthusiasm even when you fail.

Twenty years from now you will be more disappointed by the things that you didn't do than by the ones you did do. Throw off the bowlines. Sail away from the safe harbor. Catch the trade winds in your sails. Explore. Dream. Discover — Mark Twain	Explore.
Have the courage to follow your heart and intuition. They somehow already know what you want to become. — Steve Jobs	Follow your dreams.

11.1 MY QUOTE

You manage well if you achieve predefined results. Set demanding goals — and communicate them to your people over and over again. Set monthly priorities, start an immediate action plan, review weekly progress, and constantly close the gaps. Pick the right people and manage them with rewards and punishments. Build the right conditions for your people to work well: goals, organization, motivation, processes, systems, execution, and innovation. Always define who, when, what, how, and why. Finally, take true care of your people.

11.2 IT'S TIME FOR ACTION

Which quotes inspire you? What is your own quote? Write it down and live it.

References

Allen, D. (2015). *Getting Things Done.* London: Piatkus.

Dweck, C. S. (2017). *Mindset.* London: Hachette.

Hakman, K. (2017, February 24). *Steve Jobs "DRI": how to get better results everyday.* Retrieved from teamworkiq.com/steve-jobs-dri-get-better-results-everyday/: teamworkiq.com/steve-jobs-dri-get-better-results-everyday/

MindTools.com. (2018). *Theory X and Theory Y Understanding People's Motivations.* Retrieved from Mindtools: https://www.mindtools.com/pages/article/newLDR_74.htm

Vallverdú, J. (2017). *Coursera.* Retrieved from Coursera: https://www.coursera.org/lecture/emotions/protoemotions-the-holy-grail-of-protostudies-CIYCP

Printed in the United States
By Bookmasters